JAMES AITKEN WYLIE

let it SHINE

the History of the Waldenses

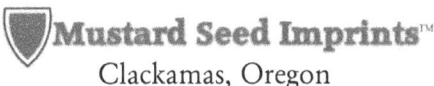
Clackamas, Oregon

let it SHINE
The History of the Waldenses

Mustard Seed Imprints
P.O. Box 1211
Clackamas, OR 97015

orders@MustardSeedImprints.com
http://www.MustardSeedImprints.com

All rights reserved. No part of this book may be used or reproduced or transmitted in any form or by any means, electronic or mechanical, including photocopying, recording, by any information storage or retrieval system without prior written permission of the publisher except for personal and classroom use and in the case of brief quotations embodied in critical articles and reviews. Making copies of any part of this book for any purpose other than your own personal and classroom use is a violation of United States copyright laws.

Copyright © 2008 Mustard Seed Imprints

First Printing

Editor: Jon D. Beaty

Cover and inside design: Jon D. Beaty

Cover Photo: iStockphoto.com

ISBN: 978-0-9817475-2-1

Contents

Preface...4
The Waldenses-Their Valleys...17
The Waldenses-Their Missions and Martyrdoms..24
First Persecutions of the Waldenses...31
Cataneo's Expedition (1488) Against the Dauphinese and Piedmontese Confessors..39
Failure of Cataneo's Expedition...48
Synod in the Waldensian Valleys...55
Persecutions and Martyrdoms..63
Preparations for a War of Extermination...74
The Great Campaign of 1561...82
Waldensian Colonies in Calabria and Apulia...93
Extinction of Waldenses in Calabria..100
The Year of the Plague...106
The Great Massacre..112
Exploits of Gianavello-Massacre and Pillage of Rora...................................126
The Exile...136
Return to the Valleys..144
Final Re-Establishment in the Valleys...151
Condition of the Waldenses From 1690...160
Epilogue..167

Preface

Amid the gloom that settled upon the earth during the long period of papal supremacy, the light of truth could not be wholly extinguished. In every age there were witnesses for God,--men who cherished faith in Christ as the only mediator between God and man, who held the Bible as the only rule of life, and who hallowed the true Sabbath. How much the world owes to these men, posterity will never know. They were branded as heretics, their motives impugned, their characters maligned, their writings suppressed, misrepresented, or mutilated. Yet they stood firm, and from age to age maintained their faith in its purity, as a sacred heritage for the generations to come.

The history of God's faithful people for hundreds of years after Rome attained to power, is known alone to heaven. They cannot be traced in human records, except as hints of their existence are found in the censures and accusations of their persecutors. It was the policy of Rome to obliterate every trace of dissent from her doctrines or decrees. Everything heretical, whether persons or writings, was destroyed. A single expression of doubt, a question as to the authority of papal dogmas, was enough to cost the life of rich or poor, high or low. Rome endeavored also to destroy every record of her cruelty toward dissenters. Papal councils decreed that books and writings containing such records should be committed to the flames. Before the invention of printing, books were few in number, and in a form not favorable for preservation; therefore there was little to prevent the Romanists from carrying out their purpose.

No church within the limits of Romish jurisdiction was long left undisturbed in the enjoyment of freedom of conscience. No sooner had the papacy obtained power than she stretched out her arms to crush all that refused to acknowledge her sway, and one after another, the churches submitted to her dominion.

In Great Britain a primitive Christianity had very early taken root. Faithful men had preached the gospel in that country with great zeal and success. Among the leading evangelists was an observer of the Bible Sabbath, and thus this truth found its way among the people for whom he labored. Toward the close of the sixth century, missionaries were sent from Rome to England to convert the barbarian Saxons. They induced many thousands to profess the Romish faith, and as the work progressed, the papal leaders and their converts encountered the primitive Christians. A striking contrast was presented. The latter were simple, humble, and scriptural in character, doctrine, and manners, while the former manifested the superstition, pomp, and arrogance of popery. The emissary of Rome demanded that these Christian churches acknowledge the supremacy of the sovereign pontiff. The Britons meekly replied that they desired to love all men, but that the pope was not entitled to supremacy in the church, and they could render to him only that submission which was due to every follower of Christ. Repeated attempts were made to secure their allegiance to Rome; but these humble Christians, amazed at the pride displayed by her apostles, steadfastly replied that they knew no other master than Christ. Now the true spirit of the papacy was revealed. Said the Romish leader, "If you will not receive brethren who bring you peace, you shall receive enemies who will bring you war. If you will not unite with us in showing the Saxons the way of life, you shall receive from them the stroke of death." These were no idle threats. War, intrigue, and deception were employed against these witnesses for a Bible faith, until the churches of Britain were destroyed, or forced to submit to the authority of the pope.

In lands beyond the jurisdiction of Rome, there existed for many centuries bodies of Christians who remained almost wholly free from papal corruption. They were surrounded by heathenism, and in the lapse of ages were affected by its errors; but they continued to regard the Bible as the only rule of faith, and adhered to many of its truths. These Christians believed in the perpetuity of the law of God, and observed the Sabbath of the fourth commandment. Churches that held to this faith and practice, existed in Central Africa and among the Armenians of Asia.

But of those who resisted the encroachments of the papal power, the Waldenses stood foremost. For centuries the churches of Piedmont maintained their independence; but the time came at last when Rome demanded their submission. After ineffectual struggles against her tyranny, the leaders of these churches reluctantly acknowledged the supremacy of the power to which the whole world seemed bowing down. A considerable number, however, refused to yield to the authority of pope or prelate. They were determined to maintain their allegiance to God, and to preserve the purity and simplicity of their faith. A separation took place. Some of the protesters crossed the Alps, and raised the standard of truth in foreign lands. Others retired into the more secluded valleys among the mountains, and there maintained their freedom to worship God.

The religious belief of the Waldenses was founded upon the written word of God, the true system of Christianity, and was in marked contrast to the errors of Rome. But those herdsmen and vine-dressers, in their obscure retreats, shut away from the world, had not themselves arrived at the truth in opposition to the dogmas and heresies of the apostate church. Theirs was not a faith newly received. Their religious belief was their inheritance from their fathers. They contended for the faith of the apostolic church, --"the faith once delivered to the saints."

Among the leading causes that had led to the separation of the true church from Rome, was the inveterate hatred of the latter toward the Bible Sabbath. As foretold by prophecy, the papal power cast down the truth to the ground. The law of God was trampled in the dust, while the traditions and customs of men were exalted. The churches that were under the rule of the papacy were early compelled to honor the Sunday as a holy day. Amid the prevailing error and superstition, many even of the true people of God, became so bewildered that while they observed the Sabbath, they refrained from labor also on the Sunday. But this did not satisfy the papal leaders. They demanded not only that Sunday be hallowed, but that the Sabbath be profaned; and they denounced in the strongest language those who dared to show it honor. It was only by fleeing from the power of Rome that any could obey God's law in peace.

The Waldenses were the first of all the peoples of Europe to obtain a translation of the Scriptures. Hundreds of years before the Reformation, they possessed the entire Bible in manuscript in their native tongue. They had the truth unadulterated, and this rendered them the special objects of hatred and persecution. They declared the Church of Rome to be the apostate Babylon of the Apocalypse, and at the peril of their lives they stood up to resist her corruptions. While, under the pressure of long-continued persecution, some compromised their faith, little by little yielding its distinctive principles, others held fast the truth. Through ages of darkness and apostasy, there were Waldenses who denied the supremacy of Rome, who rejected image worship as idolatry, and who kept the true Sabbath. Under the fiercest tempests of opposition they maintained their faith. Though gashed by the Savoyard spear, and scorched by the Romish fagot, they stood unflinchingly for God's word and his honor. They would not yield one iota of the truth.

Behind the lofty bulwarks of the mountains,--in all ages the refuge of the persecuted and oppressed,-- the Waldenses found a hiding-place. Here the lamp of truth was kept burning during the long night that descended upon Christendom. Here for a thousand years they maintained their ancient faith.

God had provided for his people a sanctuary of awful grandeur, befitting the mighty truths committed to their trust. To those faithful exiles the mountains were an emblem of the immutable righteousness of Jehovah. They pointed their children to the heights towering above them in unchanging majesty, and spoke to them of Him with whom there is no variableness nor shadow of turning, whose word is as enduring as the everlasting hills. God had set fast the mountains, and girded them with strength; no arm but that of infinite power could move them out of their place. In like manner had he established his law, the foundation of his government in Heaven and upon earth. The arm of man might reach his fellow-men and destroy their lives; but that arm could as readily uproot the mountains from their foundations, and hurl them into the sea, as it could change one precept of the law of Jehovah, or blot out one of his promises to those who do his will. In their fidelity to his law, God's servants should be as firm as the unchanging hills.

The mountains that girded their lowly valleys were a constant witness of God's creative power, and a never-failing assurance of his protecting care. Those pilgrims learned to love the silent symbols of Jehovah's presence. They indulged no repining because of the hardships of their lot; they were never lonely amid the mountain solitudes. They thanked God that he had provided for them an asylum from the wrath and cruelty of men. They rejoiced in their freedom to worship before him. Often when pursued by their enemies, the strength of the hills proved a sure defense. From many a lofty cliff they chanted the praise of God, and the armies of Rome could not silence their songs of thanksgiving.

Pure, simple, and fervent was the piety of these followers of Christ. The principles of truth they valued above houses and lands, friends, kindred, even life itself. These principles they earnestly sought to impress upon the hearts of the young. From earliest childhood the youth were instructed in the Scriptures, and taught to sacredly regard the claims of the law of God. Copies of the Bible were rare; therefore its precious words were committed to memory. Many were able to repeat large portions of both the Old and the New Testament. Thoughts of God were associated alike with the sublime scenery of nature and with the humble blessings of daily life. Little children learned to look with gratitude to God as the giver of every favor and every comfort.

Parents, tender and affectionate as they were, loved their children too wisely to accustom them to self-indulgence. Before them was a life of trial and hardship, perhaps a martyr's death. They were educated from childhood to endure hardness, to submit to control, and yet to think and act for themselves. Very early they were taught to bear responsibilities, to be guarded in speech, and to understand the wisdom of silence. One indiscreet word let fall in the hearing of their enemies, might imperil not only the life of the speaker, but the lives of hundreds of his brethren; for as wolves hunting their prey did the enemies of truth pursue those who dared to claim freedom of religious faith.

The Waldenses had sacrificed their worldly prosperity for the truth's sake, and with persevering patience they toiled for their bread. Every spot of tillable land among the mountains was carefully improved; the valleys and the less fertile hillsides were made to yield their increase. Economy and severe self-denial formed a part of the education which the children received as their only legacy. They were taught that God designs life to be a discipline, and that their wants could be supplied only by personal labor, by forethought, care, and faith. The process was laborious and wearisome, but it was wholesome, just what man needs in his fallen state, the school which God has provided for his training and development.

While the youth were inured to toil and hardship, the culture of the intellect was not neglected. They were taught that all their powers belonged to God, and that all were to be improved and developed for his service.

The church of the Alps, in its purity and simplicity, resembled the church in the first centuries. The shepherds of the flock led their charge to the fountain of living waters,--the word of God. On the grassy slopes of the valleys, or in some sheltered glen among the hills, the people gathered about the servants of Christ to listen to the words of truth.

Here the youth received instruction. The Bible was their text-book. They studied and committed to memory the words of Holy Writ. A considerable portion of their time was spent, also, in reproducing copies of the Scriptures. Some manuscripts contained the whole Bible, others only brief selections, to which some simple explanations of the text were added by those who were able to expound the Scriptures. Thus were brought forth the treasures of truth so long concealed by those who sought to exalt themselves above God.

By patient, untiring labor, sometimes in the deep, dark caverns of the earth, by the light of torches, were the Sacred Scriptures written out, verse by verse, chapter by chapter. Thus the work went on, the revealed will of God shining out like pure gold; how much brighter, clearer, and more powerful because of the trials undergone for its sake, only those could realize who were engaged in the work. Angels from Heaven surrounded these faithful workers.

Satan had urged on the papal bishops and prelates to bury the word of truth beneath the rubbish of error, heresy, and superstition; but in a most wonderful manner was it preserved uncorrupted through all the ages of darkness. It bore not the stamp of man, but the impress of God. Men have been unwearied in their efforts to obscure the plain, simple meaning of the Scriptures, and to make them contradict their own testimony; but, like the ark upon the billowy deep, the word of God outrides the storms that threaten it with destruction. As the mine has rich veins of gold and silver hidden beneath the surface, so that all must dig who would discover its precious stores, so the Holy Scriptures have treasures of truth that are unfolded only to the earnest, humble, prayerful seeker. God designed the Bible to be a lesson-book to all mankind, in childhood, youth, and manhood, and to be studied through all time. He gave his word to men as a revelation of himself. Every new truth discerned is a fresh disclosure of the character of its Author. The study of the Scriptures is the means divinely ordained to bring men into closer connection with their Creator, and to give them a clearer knowledge of his will. It is the medium of communication between God and man.

When the Waldensian youth had spent some time in their schools in the mountains, some of them were sent to complete their education in the great cities, where they could have a wider range for thought and observation than in their secluded homes. The youth thus sent forth were exposed to temptation, they witnessed vice, they encountered Satan's wily agents, who urged upon them the most subtle heresies and the most dangerous deceptions. But their education from childhood had been of a character to prepare them for all this.

In the schools whither they went, they were not to make confidants of any. Their garments were so prepared as to conceal their greatest treasure,--the precious manuscripts of the Scriptures. These, the fruit of months and years of toil, they carried with them, and whenever it could be done without exciting suspicion, they cautiously placed some portion in the way of those whose hearts seemed open to receive it. From their mother's knee the Waldensian youth had been trained with this purpose in view; they understood their work, and faithfully performed it. Converts to the true faith were won in these institutions of learning, and frequently its principles were found to be permeating the entire school; yet the papist leaders could not, by the closest inquiry, trace the so-called corrupting heresy to its source.

The Waldenses felt that God required more of them than merely to maintain the truth in their own mountains; that a solemn responsibility rested upon them to let their light shine forth to those who were in darkness; that by the mighty power of God's word, they were to break the bondage which Rome had imposed. It was a law among them that all who entered the ministry should, before taking charge of a church at home, serve three years in the missionary field. As the hands of the men of God were laid upon their heads, the youth saw before them, not the prospect of earthly wealth or glory, but possibly a martyr's fate. The missionaries began their labors in the plains and valleys at the foot of their own mountains, going forth two and two, as Jesus sent out his disciples. These co-laborers were not always together, but often met for prayer and counsel, thus strengthening each other in the faith.

To make known the nature of their mission would have insured its defeat; therefore they concealed their real character under the guise of some secular profession, most commonly that of merchants or peddlers. They offered for sale silks, jewelry, and other valuable articles, and were received as merchants where they would have been repulsed as missionaries. All the while their hearts were uplifted to God for wisdom to present a treasure more precious than gold or gems. They carried about with them portions of the Holy Scriptures concealed in their clothing or merchandise, and whenever they could do so with safety, they called the attention of the inmates of the dwelling to these manuscripts. When they saw that an interest was awakened, they left some portion with them as a gift.

With naked feet and in coarse garments, these missionaries passed through great cities, and traversed provinces far removed from their native valleys. Everywhere they scattered the precious seed. Churches sprang up in their path, and the blood of martyrs witnessed for the truth. The day of God will reveal a rich harvest of souls garnered by the labors of these faithful men. Veiled and silent, the word of God was making its way through Christendom, and meeting a glad reception in the homes and hearts of men.

To the Waldenses the Scriptures were not merely a record of God's dealings with men in the past, and a revelation of the responsibilities and duties of the present, but an unfolding of the perils and glories of the future. They believed that the end of all things was not far distant; and as they studied the Bible with prayer and tears, they were the more deeply impressed with its precious utterances, and with their duty to make known to others its saving truths. They saw the plan of salvation clearly revealed in the word of God, and they found comfort, hope, and peace in believing in Jesus. As the light illuminated their understanding and made glad their hearts, they longed to shed its beams upon those who were in the darkness of papal error.

They saw that under the guidance of pope and priests, multitudes were vainly endeavoring to obtain pardon, by afflicting their bodies for the sin of their souls. Taught to trust their good works to save them, they were ever looking to themselves, their minds dwelling upon their sinful condition, seeing themselves exposed to the wrath of God, afflicting soul and body, yet finding no relief. Thus were conscientious souls bound by the doctrines of Rome. Thousands abandoned friends and kindred, and spent their lives in convent cells. By oft-repeated fasts and cruel scourgings, by midnight vigils, by prostration for weary hours upon the cold, damp stones of their dreary abode, by long pilgrimages, by humiliating penance and fearful torture, many vainly sought to obtain peace of conscience. Oppressed with a sense of sin, and haunted with the fear of God's avenging wrath, they suffered on, until exhausted nature gave way, and without one ray of light or hope, they sank into the tomb.

The Waldenses longed to break to those starving souls the bread of life, to open to them the messages of peace in the promises of God, and to point them to Christ as their only hope of salvation. The doctrine that good works can make satisfaction for transgression of God's law, they held to be based upon falsehood. Reliance upon human merits intercepts the view of Christ's infinite love. Jesus died as men's sacrifice, because they can do nothing to recommend themselves to God. The merits of a crucified and risen Saviour are the foundation of the Christian's faith. The union of the soul to Christ by faith is as real, as close, as that of a limb to the body, or of a branch to the vine.

The teachings of popes and priests had led men to look upon the character of God, and even of Christ, as stern, gloomy, and forbidding. The Saviour of the world was represented as so far devoid of all sympathy with man in his fallen state that the mediation of priests and saints must be invoked. How those whose minds had been enlightened by the word of God longed to point these souls to Jesus as their compassionate, loving Saviour, standing with outstretched arms, inviting all to come to him with their burden of sin, their care and weariness. They longed to clear away the obstructions which Satan had piled up that men might not see the promises, and come directly to God, confessing their sins, and obtaining pardon and peace.

Eagerly did the Vaudois (vo-*dwah*) missionary unfold to the inquiring mind the precious truths of the gospel. Cautiously he produced the carefully written portions of the word of God. It was his greatest joy to give hope to the conscientious, sin-stricken soul, who could see only a God of vengeance, waiting to execute justice. With quivering lip and tearful eye did he, often on bended knees, open to his brethren the precious promises that reveal the sinner's only hope. Thus the light of truth penetrated many a darkened mind, rolling back the cloud of gloom, until the Sun of Righteousness shone into the heart with healing in his beams. Some portions of Scripture were read again and again, the hearer desiring them to be often repeated, as if he would assure himself that he had heard aright. Especially was the repetition of these words eagerly desired: "The blood of Jesus Christ his Son cleanseth us from all sin." [1 John 1:7.] "As Moses lifted up the serpent in the wilderness, even so must the Son of man be lifted up, that whosoever believeth in him should not perish, but have eternal life." [John 3:14, 15.]

Many were undeceived in regard to the claims of Rome. They saw how vain is the mediation of men or angels in behalf of the sinner. As the true light dawned upon their minds, they exclaimed with rejoicing, "Christ is my priest; his blood is my sacrifice; his altar is my confessional." They cast themselves wholly upon the merits of Jesus, repeating the words, "Without faith it is impossible to please God." [Heb. 11:6.] "There is none other name under heaven given among men, whereby we must be saved." [Acts 4:12.]

The assurance of a Saviour's love seemed too much for some of these poor tempest-tossed souls to realize. So great was the relief which it brought, such a flood of light was shed upon them, that they seemed transported to Heaven. Their hand was laid confidingly in the hand of Christ; their feet were planted upon the Rock of Ages. All fear of death was banished. They could now covet the prison and the fagot if they might thereby honor the name of their Redeemer.

In secret places the word of God was thus brought forth and read, sometimes to a single soul, sometimes to a little company who were longing for light and truth. Often the entire night was spent in this manner. So great would be the wonder and admiration of the listeners that the messenger of mercy was not infrequently compelled to cease his reading until the understanding could grasp the tidings of salvation. Often would words like these be uttered: "Will God indeed accept *my* offering? Will he smile upon *me*? Will he pardon *me*?" The answer was read, "Come unto me, all ye that labor and are heavy-laden, and I will give you rest." [Matt. 11:23.]

Faith grasps the promise, and the glad response is heard, "No more long pilgrimages to make; no more painful journeys to holy shrines. I may come to Jesus just as I am, sinful and unholy, and he will not spurn the penitential prayer. 'Thy sins be forgiven thee.' Mine, even mine, may be forgiven."

A tide of sacred joy would fill the heart, and the name of Jesus would be magnified by praise and thanksgiving. Those happy souls returned to their homes to diffuse light, to repeat to others, as well as they could, their new experience; that they had found the true and living Way. There was a strange and solemn power in the words of Scripture that spoke directly to the hearts of those who were longing for the truth. It was the voice of God, and it carried conviction to those who heard.

The messenger of truth went on his way; but his appearance of humility, his sincerity, his earnestness and deep fervor, were subjects of frequent remark. In many instances his hearers had not asked him whence he came, or whither he went. They had been so overwhelmed, at first with surprise, and afterward with gratitude and joy, that they had not thought to question him. When they had urged him to accompany them to their homes, he had replied that he must visit the lost sheep of the flock. Could he have been an angel from Heaven? they queried.

In many cases the messenger of truth was seen no more. He had made his way to other lands, he was wearing out his life in some unknown dungeon, or perhaps his bones were whitening on the spot where he had witnessed for the truth. But the words he had left behind could not be destroyed. They were doing their work in the hearts of men: the blessed results will be fully known only in the Judgment.

The Waldensian missionaries were invading the kingdom of Satan, and the powers of darkness aroused to greater vigilance. Every effort to advance the truth was watched by the prince of evil, and he excited the fears of his agents. The papal leaders saw a portent of danger to their cause from the labors of those humble itinerants. If the light of truth were allowed to shine unobstructed, it would sweep away the heavy clouds of error that enveloped the people; it would direct the minds of men to God alone, and would eventually destroy the supremacy of Rome.

The very existence of this people, holding the faith of the ancient church, was a constant testimony to Rome's apostasy, and therefore excited the most bitter hatred and persecution. Their refusal to surrender the Scriptures was also an offense that Rome could not tolerate. She determined to blot them from the earth. Now began the most terrible crusades against God's people in their mountain homes. Inquisitors were put upon their track, and the scene of innocent Abel falling before the murderous Cain was often repeated.

Again and again were their fertile lands laid waste, their dwellings and chapels swept away, so that where once were flourishing fields and the homes of an innocent, industrious people, there remained only a desert. As the ravenous beast is rendered more furious by the taste of blood, so was the rage of the papists kindled to greater intensity by the sufferings of their victims. Many of these witnesses for a pure faith were pursued across the mountains, and hunted down in the valleys where they were hidden, shut in by mighty forests, and pinnacles of rock.

No charge could be brought against the moral character of this proscribed class. Even their enemies declared them to be a peaceable, quiet, pious people. Their grand offense was that they would not worship God according to the will of the pope. For this crime, every humiliation, insult, and torture that men or devils could invent was heaped upon them.

When Rome at one time determined to exterminate the hated sect, a bull was issued by the pope condemning them as heretics, and delivering them to slaughter. They were not accused as idlers, or dishonest, or disorderly; but it was declared that they had an appearance of piety and sanctity that seduced "the sheep of the true fold." Therefore the pope ordered "that the malicious and abominable sect of malignants," if they refuse to abjure, "be crushed like venomous snakes." Did this haughty potentate expect to meet those words again? Did he know that they were registered in the books of Heaven, to confront him at the Judgment? "Inasmuch as ye have done it unto one of the least of these my brethren," said Jesus, "ye have done it unto me." [Matt. 25:40.]

This bull invited all Catholics to take up the cross against the heretics. In order to stimulate them in this cruel work, it absolved them from all ecclesiastical pains and penalties, it released all who joined the crusade from any oaths they might have taken; it legalized their title to any property which they might have illegally acquired, and promised remission of all their sins to such as should kill any heretic. It annulled all contracts made in favor of the Vaudois, ordered their domestics to abandon them, forbade all persons to give them any aid whatever, and empowered all persons to take possession of their property How clearly does this document reveal the master spirit behind the scenes! It is the roar of the dragon, and not the voice of Christ, that is heard therein.

The papal leaders would not conform their characters to the great standard of God's law, but erected a standard to suit themselves, and determined to compel all to conform to this because Rome willed it. The most horrible tragedies were enacted. Corrupt and blasphemous priests and popes were doing the work which Satan appointed them. Mercy had no place in their natures. The same spirit that crucified Christ, and that slew the apostles, the same that moved the blood-thirsty Nero against the faithful in his day, was at work to rid the earth of those who were beloved of God.

The persecutions visited for many centuries upon this God-fearing people were endured by them with a patience and constancy that honored their Redeemer. Notwithstanding the crusades against them, and the inhuman butchery to which they were subjected, they continued to send out their missionaries to scatter the precious truth. They were hunted to the death; yet their blood watered the seed sown, and it failed not of yielding fruit. Thus the Waldenses witnessed for God, centuries before the birth of Luther. Scattered over many lands, they planted the seeds of the Reformation that began in the time of Wycliffe, grew broad and deep in the days of Luther, and is to be carried forward to the close of time by those who also are willing to suffer all things for "the word of God and for the testimony of Jesus Christ." [Rev. 1:9.]

Ellen G. White
The Spirit of Prophecy Volume 4 (1884)

CHAPTER 1

The Waldenses-Their Valleys

It was the ninth century, and superstitious beliefs and idolatrous rites were overspreading the Church, when Claudius, Bishop of Turin, who was deeply imbued with the spirit of Augustine, set himself to arrest the growing corruption with all the fervor of a living faith, and the vigor of a courageous and powerful intellect. To the battle for the purity of doctrine he joined that for the independence of the Churches of Lombardy. Even in Claude's day they remained free, although many Churches more remote from Rome had already been subjugated by that all-conquering power. The Ambrosian Liturgy was still used in the cathedral of Milan, and the Augustinian doctrine continued to be preached from many of the pulpits of Lombardy and Piedmont. This independence of Rome, and this greater purity of faith and worship, these Churches mainly owed to the three Apostolic men whose names adorn their annals–Ambrose, Vigilantius, and Claude.

When Claude went to his grave, about the year 840, the battle, although not altogether dropped, was but languidly maintained. Attempts were renewed to induce the Bishops of Milan to accept the episcopal pall, the badge of spiritual vassalage, from the Pope; but it was not till the middle of the eleventh century (1059), under Nicholas II., that these attempts were successful. Petrus Damianus, Bishop of Ostia, and Anselm, Bishop of Lucca, were dispatched by the Pontiff to receive the submission of the Lombard Churches, the popular tumults amid which that submission was extorted sufficiently show that the spirit of Claude still lingered at the foot of the Alps. Nor did the clergy conceal the regret with which they surrendered their ancient liberties to a power before which the whole earth was then bowing down; for the Papal legate, Damianus, informs us that the clergy of Milan maintained in his presence that "The Ambrosian Church, according to the ancient institutions of the Fathers, was always free, without being subject to the laws of Rome, and that the Pope of Rome had no jurisdiction over their Church as to the government or constitution of it" [Petrus Damianus, Opusc., p. 5. Allix, Churches of Piedmont. p. 113. M'Crie, Hist. of Reform. in Italy, p. 2].

But if the plains were conquered, not so the mountains. A considerable body of Protesters stood out against this deed of submission. Of these some crossed the Alps, descended the Rhine, and raised the standard of opposition in the diocese of Cologne, where they were branded as Manicheans, and rewarded with the stake. Others retired into the valleys of the Piedmontese Alps, and there maintained their scriptural faith and their ancient independence. What has just been related respecting the dioceses of Milan and Turin settles the question of the apostolicity of the Churches of the Waldensian valleys. It is not necessary to show that missionaries were sent from Rome in the first age to plant Christianity in these valleys, nor is it necessary to show that these Churches have existed as distinct and separate communities from early days; enough that they formed a part, as unquestionably they did, of the great evangelical Church of the North of Italy. This is the proof at once of their apostolicity and their independence. It attests their descent from apostolic men, if doctrine be the life of Churches. When their co-religionists on the plains entered within the pale of the Roman jurisdiction, they retired within the mountains, and, spurning alike the tyrannical yoke and the corrupt tenets of the Church of the Seven Hills, they preserved in its purity and simplicity the faith their fathers had handed down to them. Rome manifestly was the schismatic, she it was that had abandoned what was once the common faith of Christendom, leaving by that step to all who remained on the old ground the indisputably valid title of the True Church.

Behind this rampart of mountains, which Providence, foreseeing the approach of evil days, would almost seem to have reared on purpose, did the remnant of the early apostolic Church of Italy kindle their lamp, and here did that lamp continue to burn all through the long night which descended on Christendom. There is a singular concurrence of evidence in favor of their high antiquity. Their traditions invariably point to an unbroken descent from the earliest times, as regards their religious belief. The Nobla Leycon, which dates from the year 1100 [recent German criticism refers the Nobla Leycon to a later date, but still one anterior to the Reformation], goes to prove that the Waldenses of Piedmont did not owe their rise to Peter Waldo of Lyons, who did not appear till the latter half of that century (1169). The Nobla Leycon though a poem, is in reality a confession of faith, and could have been composed only after some considerable study of the system of Christianity, in contradistinction to the errors of Rome. How could a Church have arisen with such a document in her hands? Or how could these herdsmen and vine-dressers, shut up in their mountains, have detected the errors against which they bore testimony, and found their way to the truths of which they made open profession in times of darkness like these? If we grant that their religious beliefs were the heritage of former ages, handed down from an evangelical ancestry, all is plain; but if we maintain that they were the discovery of the men of those days, we assert what approaches almost to a miracle. Their greatest enemies, Claude Seyssel of Turin (1517), and Reynerius the Inquisitor (1250), have admitted their antiquity, and stigmatized them as "the most dangerous of all heretics, because the most ancient."

Rorenco, Prior of St. Roch, Turin (1640), was employed to investigate the origin and antiquity of the Waldenses, and of course had access to all the Waldensian documents in the ducal archives, and being their bitter enemy he may be presumed to have made his report not more favorable than he could help. Yet he states that "they were not a new sect in the ninth and tenth centuries, and that Claude of Turin must have detached them from the Church in the ninth century."

Within the limits of her own land did God provide a dwelling for this venerable Church. Let us bestow a glance upon the region. As one comes from the south, across the level plain of Piedmont, while yet nearly a hundred miles off, one sees the Alps rise before one, stretching like a great wall along the horizon. From the gates of the morning to those of the setting sun, the mountains run on in a line of towering magnificence. Pasturages and chestnut-forests clothe their base; eternal snows crown their summits. How varied are their forms! Some rise like castles of stupendous strength; others shoot up tall and tapering like needles; while others again run along in serrated lines, their summits torn and cleft by the storms of many thousand winters. At the hour of sunrise, what a glory kindles along the crest of that snowy rampart! At sunset the spectacle is again renewed, and a line of pyres is seen to burn in the evening sky.

Drawing nearer the hills, on a line about thirty miles west of Turin, there opens before one what seems a great mountain portal. This is the entrance to the Waldensian territory. A low hill drawn along in front serves as a defense against all who may come with hostile intent, as but too frequently happened in times gone by, while a stupendous monolith-the Castelluzzo-shoots up to the clouds, and stands sentinel at the gate of this renowned region. As one approaches La Torre the Castelluzzo rises higher and higher, and irresistibly fixes the eye by the perfect beauty of its pillar-like form. [The new and elegant temple of the Waldenses now rises near the foot of the Castelluzzo.] But to this mountain a higher interest belongs than any that mere symmetry can give it. It is indissolubly linked with martyr-memories, and borrows a halo from the achievements of the past. How often, in days of old, was the confessor hurled sheer down its awful steep, and dashed on the rocks at its foot! And there, commingled in one ghastly heap, growing ever the bigger and ghastlier as another and yet another victim was added to it, lay the mangled bodies of pastor and peasant, of mother and child! It was the tragedies connected with this mountain mainly that called forth Milton's noble sonnet:

> "Avenge, O Lord, Thy slaughtered saints, whose bones
> Lie scattered on the Alpine mountains cold.
> Who were Thy sheep, and in their ancient fold,
> Slain by the bloody Piedmonteses, that rolled
> Mother with infant down the rocks. Their moans
> The vales redoubled to the hills, and they
> To heaven."

The Waldensian valleys are seven in number; they were more in ancient times, but the limits of the Vandois territory have undergone repeated curtailment, and now only seven remain, lying between Pinerolo on the east and Monte Viso on the west-that pyramidal hill which forms so prominent an object from every part of the plain of Piedmont, towering as it does above the surrounding mountains, and, like a horn of silver, cutting the ebon of the firmament.

The first three valleys run out somewhat like the spokes of a wheel, the spot on which we stand-the gateway, namely-being the nave. The first is Luserna, or Valley of Light. It runs right out in a grand gorge of some twelve miles in length by about two in width. It wears a carpeting of meadows, which the waters of the Pelice keep ever fresh and bright. A profusion of vines, acacias, and mulberry-trees, fleck it with their shadows; and a wall of lofty mountains encloses it on either hand. The second is Rora, or Valley of Dews. It is a vast cup, some fifty miles in circumference, its sides luxuriantly clothed with meadow and corn-field, with fruit and forest trees, and its rim formed of craggy and peaked mountains, many of them snow-clad. The third is Angrogna, or Valley of Groans. Of it we shall speak more particularly afterwards. Beyond the extremity of the first three valleys are the remaining four, forming, as it were, the rim of the wheel. These last are enclosed in their turn by a line of lofty mountains, which form a wall of defense around the entire territory. Each valley is a fortress having its own gate of ingress and egress, with its caves, and rocks, and mighty chestnut-trees, forming places of retreat and shelter, so that the highest engineering skill could not have better adapted each several valley to this very purpose. It is not less remarkable that, taking all these valleys together, each is so related to each, the one opening into the other, that they may be said to form one fortress of amazing and matchless strength-wholly impregnable, in fact. All the fortresses of Europe, though combined, would not form a citadel so enormously strong, and so dazzlingly magnificent, as the mountain dwelling of the Vandois. "The Eternal, our God," says Leger, "having destined this land to be the theatre of his marvels, and the bulwark of his ark, has, by natural means, most marvelously fortified it." The battle begun in one valley could be continued in another, and carried round the entire territory, till at last the invading foe, overpowered by the rocks rolled upon him from the mountains, or assailed by enemies which would start suddenly out of the mist or issue from some unsuspected cave, found retreat impossible, and, cut off in detail, left his bones to whiten the mountains he had come to subdue.

These valleys are lovely and fertile, as well as strong. They are watered by numerous torrents, which descend from the snows of the summits. The grassy carpet of their bottom; the mantling vine and the golden grain of their lower slopes;

the chalets that dot their sides, sweetly embowered amid fruit-trees; and, higher up, the great chestnut-forests and the pasture-lands, where the herdsmen keep watch over their flocks all through the summer days and the starlit nights: the nodding crags, from which the torrent leaps into the light; the rivulet, singing with quiet gladness in the shady nook; the mists, moving grandly among the mountains, now veiling, now revealing, their majesty; and the far-off summits, tipped with silver, to be changed at eve into gleaming gold-make up a picture of blended beauty and grandeur, not equaled, perhaps, and certainly not surpassed, in any other region of the earth.

In the heart of their mountains is situated the most interesting, perhaps, of all their valleys. It was in this retreat, walled round by "hills whose heads touch heaven," that their barbes or pastors, from all their several parishes, were wont to meet in annual synod. It was here that their college stood, and it was here that their missionaries were trained, and, after ordination, were sent forth to sow the good seed, as opportunity offered, in other lands. Let us visit this valley. We ascend to it by the long, narrow, and winding Angrogna. Bright meadows enliven its entrance. The mountains on either hand are clothed with the vine, the mulberry, and the chestnut. Anon the valley contracts. It becomes rough with projecting rocks, and shady with great trees. A few paces farther, and it expands into a circular basin, feathery with birches, musical with falling waters, environed atop by naked crags, fringed with dark pines, while the white peak looks down out of heaven. A little in advance the valley seems shut in by a mountainous wall, drawn right across it; and beyond, towering sublimely upward, is seen an assemblage of snow-clad Alps, amid which is placed the valley we are in quest of, where burned of old the candle of the Waldenses. Some terrible convulsion has rent this mountain from top to bottom, opening a path through it to the valley beyond. We enter the dark chasm, and proceed along on a narrow ledge in the mountain's side, hung half-way between the torrent, which is heard thundering in the abyss below, and the summits which lean over us above. Journeying thus for about two miles, we find the pass beginning to widen, the light to break in, and now we arrive at the gate of the Pra.

There opens before us a noble circular valley, its grassy bottom watered by torrents, its sides dotted with dwellings and clothed with corn-fields and pasturages, with a ring of white peaks encircling it above. This was the inner sanctuary of the Waldensian temple. The rest of Italy had turned aside to idols, the Waldensian territory alone had been reserved for the worship of the true God. And was it not meet that on its native soil a remnant of the Apostolic Church of Italy should be maintained, that Rome and all Christendom might have before their eyes a perpetual monument of what they themselves had once been, and a living witness to testify how far they had departed from their first faith?[1]

ENDNOTES:

[1] This short description of the Waldensian valleys is drawn from the author's personal observations.

CHAPTER 2

The Waldenses–Their Missions and Martyrdoms

One would like to have a near view of the barbes or pastors, who presided over the school of early Protestant theology that existed in the valleys, and to know how it fared with evangelical Christianity in the ages that preceded the Reformation. But the time is remote, and the events are dim. We can but doubtfully glean from a variety of sources the facts necessary to form a picture of this venerable Church, and even then the picture is not complete. The theology of which this was one of the fountain-heads was not the clear, well-defined, and comprehensive system which the sixteenth century gave us; it was only what the faithful men of the Lombard Churches had been able to save from the wreck of primitive Christianity. True religion, being a revelation, was from the beginning complete and perfect; nevertheless, in this as in every other branch of knowledge, it is only by patient labor that man is able to extricate and arrange all its parts, and to come into the full possession of truth. The theology taught in former ages in the peak-environed valley in which we have in imagination placed ourselves was drawn from the Bible. The atoning death and justifying righteousness of Christ was its cardinal truth. This, the Nobla Leycon [Noble Lesson] and other ancient documents abundantly testify. The Nobla Leycon sets forth with tolerable clearness the doctrine of the Trinity, the fall of man, the incarnation of the Son, the perpetual authority of the Decalogue as given by God [this disproves the charge of Manichaeism brought against them by their enemies], the need of Divine grace in order to do good works, the necessity of holiness, the institution of the ministry, the resurrection of the body, and the eternal bliss of heaven. [Sir Samuel Morland gives the Nobla Leycon in full in his History of the Churches of the Waldenses. Allix (chap. 18) gives a summary of it.] This creed its professors exemplified in lives of evangelical virtue. The blamelessness of the Waldenses passed into a proverb, so that one more than ordinarily exempt from the vices of his time was sure to be suspected of being a Vaudes. [The Nobla Leycon has the following passage:--"If there be an honest man, who desires to love God and fear Jesus Christ, who will neither slander, nor swear, nor lie, nor commit adultery, nor kill, nor steal, nor avenge himself of his enemies, they presently say of such a one he is a Vaudes, and worthy of death."]

If doubt there were regarding the tenets of the Waldenses, the charges which their enemies have preferred against them would set that doubt at rest, and make it tolerably certain that they held substantially what the apostles before their day, and the Reformers after it, taught. The indictment against the Waldenses included a formidable list of "heresies." They held that there had been no true Pope since the days of Sylvester; that temporal offices and dignities were not meet for preachers of the Gospel; that the Pope's pardons were a cheat; that purgatory was a fable; that relics were simply rotten bones which had belonged to one knew not whom; that to go on pilgrimage served no end, save to empty one's purse; that flesh might be eaten any day if one's appetite served him; that holy water was not a whit more efficacious than rain-water; and that prayer in a barn was just as effectual as if offered in a church. They were accused, moreover, of having scoffed at the doctrine of transubstantiation, and of having spoken blasphemously of Rome as the harlot of the Apocalypse. [See a list of numerous heresies and blasphemies charged upon the Waldenses by the Inquisitor-Reynerius, who wrote about the year 1250, and extracted by Allix (chap. 22).]

There is reason to believe, from recent historical researches, that the Waldenses possessed the New Testament in the vernacular. The "Lingua Romana," or Romaunt tongue, was the common language of the south of Europe from the eighth to the fourteenth century. It was the language of the troubadours and of men of letters in the Dark Ages. Into this tongue-the Romaunt-was the first translation of the whole of the New Testament made so early as the twelfth century. This fact Dr. Gilly has been at great pains to prove in his work, The Romaunt Version of the

Gospel according to John. [The Romaunt Version of the Gospel according to John, from MS. preserved in Trinity College, Dublin, and in the Bibliotheque du Roi, Paris. By William Stephen Gilly, D.D., Canon of Durham, and Vicar of Norham. Lond., 1848.] The sum of what Dr. Gilly, by a patient investigation into facts, and a great array of historic documents, maintains, is that all the books of the New Testament were translated from the Latin Vulgate into the Romaunt, that this was the first literal version since the fall of the empire, that it was made in the twelfth century, and was the first translation available for popular use. There were numerous earlier translations, but only of parts of the Word of God, and many of these were rather paraphrases or digests of Scripture than translations, and, moreover, they were so bulky, and by consequence so costly, as to be utterly beyond the reach of the common people. This Romaunt version was the first complete and literal translation of the New Testament of Holy Scripture; it was made, as Dr. Gilly, by a chain of proofs, shows, most probably under the superintendence and at the expense of Peter Waldo of Lyons, not later than 1180, and so is older than any complete version in German, French, Italian, Spanish, or English. This version was widely spread in the south of France, and in the cities of Lombardy. It was in common use among the Waldenses of Piedmont, and it was no small part, doubtless, of the testimony borne to truth by these mountaineers to preserve and circulate it. Of the Romaunt New Testament six copies have come down to our day. A copy is preserved at each of the four following places: Lyons, Grenoble, Zurich, Dublin; and two copies at Paris. These are small, plain, and portable volumes, contrasting with those splendid and ponderous folios of the Latin Vulgate, penned in characters of gold and silver, richly illuminated, their bindings decorated with gems, inviting admiration rather than study, and unfitted by their size and splendor for the use of the people.

The Church of the Alps, in the simplicity of its constitution, may be held to have been a reflection of the Church of the first centuries. The entire territory included in the Waldensian limits was divided into parishes. In each parish was placed a pastor, who led his flock to the living waters of the Word of God. He preached, he dispensed the Sacraments, he visited the sick, and catechized the young. With him was associated in the government of his congregation a consistory of laymen. The synod met once a year. It was composed of all the pastors, with an equal number of laymen, and its most frequent place of meeting was the secluded mountain-engirdled valley at the head of Angrogna. Sometimes as many as a hundred and fifty barbes, with the same number of lay members, would assemble. We can imagine them seated-it may be on the grassy slopes of the valley-a venerable company of humble, learned, earnest men, presided over by a simple moderator (for higher office or authority was unknown amongst them), and suspending their deliberations respecting the affairs of their Churches, and the condition of their flocks, only to offer their prayers and praises to the Eternal, while the majestic snow-clad peaks looked down upon them from the silent firmament. There needed, verily, no magnificent fane, no blazonry of mystic rites to make their assembly august.

The youth who here sat at the feet of the more venerable and learned of their barbes used as their text-book the Holy Scriptures. And not only did they study the sacred volume; they were required to commit to memory, and be able accurately to recite, whole Gospels and Epistles. This was a necessary accomplishment on the part of public instructors in those ages when printing was unknown, and copies of the Word of God were rare. Part of their time was occupied in transcribing the Holy Scriptures, or portions of them, which they were to distribute when they went forth as missionaries. By this, and by other agencies, the seed of the Divine Word was scattered throughout Europe more widely than is commonly supposed. To this a variety of causes contributed. There was then a general impression that the world was soon to end. Men thought that they saw the prognostications of its dissolution in the disorder into which all things had fallen. The pride, luxury, and profligacy of the clergy, led not a few laymen to ask if better and more certain guides were not to be had. Many of the troubadours were religious men, whose lays were sermons. The hour of deep and universal slumber had passed; the serf was contending with his seigneur for personal freedom, and the city was waging war with the baronial castle for civic and corporate independence. The New Testament-and, as we learn from incidental notices, portions of the Old-coming at this juncture in a language understood alike in the court as in the camp, in the city as in the rural hamlet, was welcome to many, and its truths obtained a wider promulgation than perhaps had taken place since the publication of the Vulgate by Jerome.

After passing a certain time in the school of the barbes, it was not uncommon for the Waldensian youth to proceed to the seminaries in the great cities of Lombardy, or to the Sorbonne at Paris. There they saw other customs, were initiated into other studies, and had a wider horizon around them than in the seclusion of their native valleys. Many of them became expert dialecticians, and often made converts of the rich merchants with whom they traded, and the landlords in whose houses they lodged. The priests seldom cared to meet in argument the Waldensian missionary.

To maintain the truth in their own mountains was not the only object of this people. They felt their relations to the rest of Christendom. They sought to drive back the darkness, and re-conquer the kingdom which Rome had overwhelmed. They were an evangelistic as well as an evangelical Church. It was an old law among them that all who took orders in their Church should, before being eligible to a home charge, serve three years in the mission field. The youth on whose head the assembled barbes laid their hands saw in prospect not a rich benefice, but a possible martyrdom. The ocean they did not cross. Their mission field was the realms that lay outspread at the foot of their own mountains. They went forth two and two, concealing their real character under the guise of a secular profession, most commonly that of merchants or peddlers. They carried silks, jewelry, and other articles, at that time not easily purchasable save at distant mart, and they were welcomed as merchants where they would have been spurned as missionaries. The door of the cottage and the portal of the baron's castle stood equally open to them. But their address was mainly shown in selling, without money and without price, rarer and more valuable merchandise than the gems and silks which had procured them entrance. They took care to carry with them, concealed among their wares or about their persons, portions of the Word of God, their own transcription commonly, and to this they would draw the attention of the inmates. When they saw a desire to possess it, they would freely make a gift of it where the means of purchase were absent.

There was no kingdom of Southern and Central Europe to which these missionaries did not find their way, and where they did not leave traces of their visit in the disciples whom they made. On the west they penetrated into Spain. In

Southern France they found congenial fellow-laborers in the Albigenses, by whom the seeds of truth were plentifully scattered over Dauphine and Languedoc. On the east, descending the Rhine and the Danube, they leavened Germany, Bohemia, and Poland with their doctrines, their track being marked with the edifices for worship and the stakes of martyrdom that arose around their steps. [Stranski, apud, Lenfant's Concile de Constance, quoted by Count Valerian Krasinski in his History of the Rise, Progress, and Decline of the Reformation in Poland, vol. i., p. 53; Lond., 1838. Illyricus Flaccius, in his Catalogus Testium Veritatis (Amstelodami, 1679), says: "Pars Valdensium in Germaniam transiit atque apud Bohemos in Polonia ac Livonia sedem fixit." Leger says that the Waldenses had, about the year 1210, Churches in Slavonia, Sarmatia, and Livonia. (Histoire Generale des Eglises Evangeliques des Vallees du Piedmont ou Vaudois, vol. ii., pp. 336,337; 1669.)] Even the Seven-hilled City they feared not to enter, scattering the seed on ungenial soil, if perchance some of it might take root and grow. Their naked feet and coarse woolen garments made them somewhat marked figures, in the streets of a city that clothed itself in purple and fine linen; and when their real errand was discovered, as sometimes chanced, the rulers of Christendom took care to further, in their own way, the springing of the seed, by watering it with the blood of the men who had sowed it [McCrie, Hist. Ref. in Italy, p. 4].

Thus did the Bible in those ages, veiling its majesty and its mission, travel silently through Christendom, entering homes and hearts, and there making its abode. From her lofty seat Rome looked down with contempt upon the Book and its humble bearers. She aimed at bowing the necks of kings, thinking if they were obedient meaner men would not dare revolt, and so she took little heed of a power which, weak as it seemed, was destined at a future day to break in pieces the fabric of her dominion. By-and-by she began to be uneasy, and to have a boding of calamity. The penetrating eye of Innocent III detected the quarter whence danger was to arise. He saw in the labors of these humble men the beginning of a movement which, if permitted to go on and gather strength, would one day sweep away all that it had taken the toils and intrigues of centuries to achieve. He straightway commenced those terrible crusades which wasted the sowers but watered the seed, and helped to bring on, at its appointed hour, the catastrophe which he sought to avert.

CHAPTER 3
First Persecutions of the Waldenses

The Waldenses stand apart and alone in the Christian world. Their place on the surface of Europe is unique; their position in history is not less unique; and the end appointed them to fulfill is one which has been assigned to them alone, no other people being permitted to share it with them.

The Waldenses bear a twofold testimony. Like the snow-clad peaks amid which their dwelling is placed, which look down upon the plains of Italy on the one side, and the provinces of France on the other, this people stand equally related to primitive ages and modern times, and give by no means equivocal testimony respecting both Rome and the Reformation. If they are old, then Rome is new; if they are pure, then Rome is corrupt; and if they have retained the faith of the apostles, it follows incontestably that Rome has departed from it. That the Waldensian faith and worship existed many centuries before Protestantism arose is undeniable; the proofs and monuments of this fact lie scattered over all the histories and all the lands of mediaeval Europe; but the antiquity of the Waldenses is the antiquity of Protestantism. The Church of the Reformation was in the loins of the Waldensian Church ages before the birth of Luther; her first cradle was placed amid those terrors and sublimities, those ice-clad peaks and great bulwarks of rock. In their dispersions over so many lands-over France, the Low Countries, Germany, Poland, Bohemia, Moravia, England, Calabria, Naples-the Waldenses sowed the seeds of that great spiritual revival which, beginning in the days of

Wycliffe, and advancing in the times of Luther and Calvin, awaits its full consummation in the ages to come.

In the place which the Church of the Alps has held, and the office she has discharged, we see the reason of that peculiar and bitter hostility which Rome has ever borne this holy and venerable community. It was natural that Rome should wish to efface so conclusive a proof of her apostasy, and silence a witness whose testimony so emphatically corroborates the position of Protestantism. The great bulwark of the Reformed Church is the Word of God; but next to this is the pre-existence of a community spread throughout Western Christendom, with doctrines and worship substantially one with those of the Reformation.

The persecutions of this remarkable people form one of the most heroic pages of the Church's history. These persecutions, protracted through many centuries, were endured with a patience, a constancy, a bravery, honorable to the Gospel as well as to those simple people, whom the Gospel converted into heroes and martyrs. Their resplendent virtues illumined the darkness of their age; and we turn with no little relief from a Christendom sunk in barbarism and superstition to this remnant of an ancient people, who here in their mountain-engirdled territory practiced the simplicity, the piety, and the heroism of a better age. It is the main object of this work to deal with those persecutions of the Waldenses which connect themselves with the Reformation and which were, in fact, part of that mighty effort made by Rome to extinguish Protestantism. But we must introduce ourselves to the great tragedy by a brief notice of the attacks which led up to it.

That part of the Alpine chain which extends between Turin on the east and Grenoble on the west is known as the Cottian Alps. This is the dwelling-place of the Waldenses, the land of ancient Protestantism. On the west the mountains slope towards the plains of France, and on the east they run down to those of Piedmont. That line of glittering summits, conspicuous among which is the lofty snow-clad peak of Monte Viso on the west, and the craggy escarpments of Genevre on the east, forms the boundary between the Albigenses and the Waldenses, the two bodies of these early witnesses. On the western slope were the dwellings of the former people, and on the eastern those of the latter. Not entirely so, however, for the Waldenses, crossing the summits, had taken possession of the more elevated portion of the western declivities, and scarcely was there a valley in which their villages and sanctuaries were not to be found. But in the lower valleys, and more particularly in the vast and fertile plains of Dauphine and Provence, spread out at the foot of the Alps, the inhabitants were mainly of cis-Alpine or Gallic extraction, and are known in history as the Albigenses. How flourishing they were, how numerous and opulent their towns, how rich their corn-fields and vineyards, and how polished the manners and cultured the genius of the people, we have already said. Innocent III exacted a terrible expiation of them for their attachment to a purer Christianity than that of Rome. He launched his bull; he sent forth his inquisitors; and soon the fertility and beauty of the region were swept away; city and sanctuary sank in ruins; and the plains so recently covered with smiling fields were converted into a desert. The work of destruction had been done with tolerable completeness on the west of the Alps; and after a short pause it was commenced on the east, it being resolved to pursue these confessors of a pure faith across the mountains, and attack them in those grand valleys which open into Italy, where they lay entrenched, as it were, amid dense chestnut forests and mighty pinnacles of rock.

We place ourselves at the foot of the eastern declivity, about thirty miles to the west of Turin. Behind us is the vast sweep of the plain of Piedmont. Above us in front tower the Alps, here forming a crescent of grand mountains, extending from the escarped summit that leans over Pinerolo on the right, to the pyramidal peak of Monte Viso, which cleaves the ebon like a horn of silver, and marks the farthest limit of the Waldensian territory on the left. In the bosom of that mountain crescent, shaded by its chestnut forests, and encircled by its glittering peaks, are hung the famous valleys of that people whose martyrdoms we are now to narrate.

In the centre of the picture, right before us, rises the pillar-like Castelluzzo; behind it is the towering mass of the Vandalin; and in front, as if to bar the way against the entrance of any hostile force into this sacred territory, is drawn the long, low hill of Bricherasio, feathery with woods, bristling with great rocks, and leaving open, between its rugged mass and the spurs of Monte Friolante on the west, only a narrow avenue, shaded by walnut and acacia trees, which leads up to the point where the valleys, spreading out fan-like, bury themselves in the mountains that open their stony arms to receive them. Historians have enumerated some thirty persecutions enacted on this little spot.

One of the earliest dates in the martyr-history of this people is 1332, or thereabouts, for the time is not distinctly marked. The reigning Pope was John XXII. Desirous of resuming the work of Innocent III, he ordered the inquisitors to repair to the Valleys of Lucerna and Perosa, and execute the laws of the Vatican against the heretics that peopled them. What success attended the expedition is not known, and we instance it chiefly on this account, that the bull commanding it bears undesigned testimony to the then flourishing condition of the Waldensian Church, inasmuch as it complains that synods, which the Pope calls "chapters," were wont to assemble in the Valley of Angrogna, attended by 500 delegates. [Compare Antoine Monastier, History of the Vaudois Church, p. 121 (Lond., 1848), with Alexis Muston, Israel of the Alps, p. 8 (Lond., 1852).] This was before Wycliffe had begun his career in England.

After this date scarcely was there a Pope who did not bear unintentional testimony to their great numbers and wide diffusion. In 1352 we find Pope Clement VI charging the Bishop of Embrun, with whom he associates a Francisan friar and inquisitor, to essay the purification of those parts adjoining his diocese which were known to be infected with heresy. The territorial lords and city syndies were invited to aid him. While providing for the heretics of the Valleys, the Pope did not overlook those farther off. He urged the Dauphin, Charles of France, and Louis, King of Naples, to seek out and punish those of their subjects who had strayed from their faith. Clement referred doubtless to the Vaudois colonies, which are known to have existed in that age at Naples. The fact that the heresy of the Waldensian mountains extended to the plains at their feet, is attested by the letter of the Pope to Joanna, wife of the King of Naples, who owned lands in the Marquisate of Saluzzo, near the Valleys, urging her to purge her territory of the heretics that lived in it [Monastier, Hist. Vaudois Church p. 123].

The zeal of the Pope, however, was but indifferently seconded by that of the secular lords. The men they were enjoined to exterminate were the most industrious and peaceable of their subjects; and willing as they no doubt were to oblige the Pope, they were naturally averse to incur so great a loss as would be caused by the destruction of the flower of their populations. Besides, the princes of that age were often at war among themselves, and had not much leisure or inclination to make war on the Pope's behalf. Therefore the Papal thunder sometimes rolled harmlessly over the Valleys, and the mountain-home of these confessors was wonderfully shielded till very nearly the era of the Reformation. We find Gregory XI, in 1373, writing to Charles V of France, to complain that his officers thwarted his inquisitors in Dauphine; that the Papal judges were not permitted to institute proceedings against the suspected without the consent of the civil judge; and that the disrespect to the spiritual tribunal was sometimes carried so far as to release condemned heretics from prison [Monastier, p. 123]. Notwithstanding this leniency-so culpable in the eyes of Rome-on the part of princes and magistrates, the inquisitors were able to make not a few victims. These acts of violence provoked reprisals at times on the part of the Waldenses. On one occasion (1375) the Popish city of Susa was attacked, the Dominican convent forced, and the inquisitor put to death. Other Dominicans were called to expiate their rigor against the Vaudois with the penalty of their lives. An obnoxious inquisitor of Turin is said to have been slain on the highway near Bricherasio [Ibid.].

There came evil days to the Popes themselves. First, they were chased to Avignon; next, the yet greater calamity of the "schism" befell them; but their own afflictions had not the effect of softening their hearts towards the confessors of the Alps. During the clouded era of their "captivity," and the tempestuous days of the schism, they pursued with the same inflexible rigor their policy of extermination. They were ever and anon fulminating their persecuting edicts, and their inquisitors were scouring the Valleys in pursuit of victims. An inquisitor of the name of Borelli had 150 Vaudois men, besides a great number of women, girls, and even young children, brought to Grenoble and burned alive [Monastier, p. 123].

The closing days of the year 1400 witnessed a terrible tragedy, the memory of which has not been obliterated by the many greater which have followed it. The scene of this catastrophe was the Valley of Pragelas, one of the higher reaches of Perosa, which opens near Pinerolo, and is watered by the Clusone. It was the Christmas of 1400, and the inhabitants dreaded no attack, believing themselves sufficiently protected by the snows which then lay deep on their mountains. They were destined to experience the bitter fact that the rigors of the season had not quenched the fire of their persecutor's malice. Borelli, at the head of an armed troop, broke suddenly into Pragelas, meditating the entire extinction of its population. The miserable inhabitants fled in haste to the mountains, carrying on their shoulders their old men, their sick, and their infants, knowing what fate awaited them should they leave them behind. In their flight a great many were overtaken and slain. Nightfall brought them deliverance from the pursuit, but no deliverance from horrors not less dreadful. The main body of the fugitives wandered in the direction of Macel, in the storm-swept and now ice-clad valley of San Martino, where they encamped on a summit which has ever since, in memory of the event, borne the name of the Alberge or Refuge. Without shelter, without food, the frozen snow around them, the winter's sky overhead, their sufferings were inexpressibly great. When morning broke what a heartrending spectacle did day disclose! Some of the miserable group lost their hands and feet from frostbite; while others were stretched out on the snow, stiffened corpses. Fifty young children, some say eighty, were found dead with cold, some lying on the bare ice, others locked in the frozen arms of their mothers, who had perished on that dreadful night along with their babes. In the Valley of Pragelas, to this day, sire recites to son the tale of that Christmas tragedy. [Histoire Generale des Eglises Evangeliques des Vallees de Piedmont, ou Vaudoises. Par Jean Leger. Part ii., pp. 6,7. Leyden, 1669. Monastier, pp. 123,124].

It was the year 1487. A great blow was meditated. The process of purging the Valleys languished. Pope Innocent VIII, who then filled the Papal chair, remembered how his renowned namesake, Innocent III, by an act of summary vengeance, had swept the Albigensian heresy from the south of France. Imitating the vigor of his predecessor, he would purge the Valleys as effectually and as speedily as Innocent III had done the plains of Dauphine and Provence.

The first step of the Pope was to issue a bull, denouncing as heretical those whom he delivered over to slaughter. This bull, after the manner of all such documents, was expressed in terms as sanctimonious as its spirit was inexorably cruel. It brings no charge against these men, as lawless, idle, dishonest, or disorderly; their fault was that they did not worship as Innocent worshipped, and that they practiced a "simulated sanctity," which had the effect of seducing the sheep of the true fold, therefore he orders "that malicious and abominable sect of malignants," if they "refuse to abjure, to be crushed like venomous snakes." [The bull is given in full in Leger, who also says that he had made a faithful copy of it, and lodged it with other documents in the University Library of Cambridge. (Hist. Gen. des Eglises Vaud., part ii., pp. 7-15.)]

To carry out his bull, Innocent VIII appointed Albert Cataneo, Archdeacon of Cremona, his legate, entrusting to him the chief conduct of the enterprise. He fortified him, moreover, with Papal missives to all princes, dukes, and powers, within whose dominions any Vaudois were to be found. The Pope especially accredited him to Charles VIII of France and Charles II of Savoy, commanding them to support him with the whole power of their arms. The bull invited all Catholics to take up the cross against the heretics; and to stimulate them in this pious work it "absolved from all ecclesiastical pains and penalties, general and particular; it released all who joined the crusade from any oaths they might have taken; it legitimatized their title to any property they might have illegally acquired; and promised remission of all their sins to such as should kill any heretic. It annulled all contracts made in favor of Vaudois, ordered their domestics to abandon them, forbade all persons to give them any aid whatever, and empowered all persons to take possession of their property."

These were powerful incentives--plenary pardon and unrestrained license. They were hardly needed to awaken the zeal of the neighboring populations, always too ready to show their devotion to Rome by spilling the blood and making a booty of the goods of the Waldenses. The King of France and the Duke of Savoy lent a willing ear to the summons from the Vatican. They made haste to unfurl their banners, and enlist soldiers in this holy cause, and soon a numerous army was on its march to sweep from the mountains where they had dwelt from immemorial time, these confessors of the Gospel faith pure and undefiled. In the train of this armed host came a motley crowd of volunteers, "vagabond adventurers," says Muston, "ambitious fanatics, reckless pillagers, merciless assassins, assembled from all parts of Italy"*--a horde of brigands in short, the worthy tools of the man whose bloody work they were assembled to do [Muston, Israel of the Alps, p. 10].

Before all these arrangements were finished it was the month of June of 1488. The Pope's bull was talked of in all countries: and the din of preparation rung far and near, for it was not only on the Waldensian mountains, but on the Waldensian race, wherever dispersed, in Germany, in Calabria, and in other countries, that this terrible blow was to fall [Leger, Livr. ii., p. 7]. All kings were invited to gird on the sword, and come to the help of the Church in the execution of her purpose of effecting an extermination of her enemies that should never need to be repeated. Wherever a Vaudois foot trod, the soil was polluted, and had to be cleansed; wherever a Vaudois breathed, the air was tainted, and must be purified; wherever Vaudois psalm or prayer ascended, there was the infection of heresy, and around the spot a cordon must be drawn to protect the spiritual health of the district. The Pope's bull was thus universal in its application, and almost the only people left ignorant of the commotion it had excited, and the bustle of preparation it had called forth, were those poor men on whom this terrible tempest was about to burst.

The joint army numbered about 18,000 regular soldiers. This force was swelled by the thousands of ruffians, already mentioned, drawn together by the spiritual and temporal rewards to be earned in this work of combined piety and pillage [Leger, livr. ii., p. 26]. The Piedmontese division of this host directed their course towards the "Valleys" proper, on the Italian side of the Alps. The French division, marching from the north, advanced to attack the inhabitants of the Dauphinese Alps, where the Albigensian heresy, recovering somewhat its terrible excision by Innocent III, had begun again to take root. Two storms, from opposite points, or rather from all points, were approaching those mighty mountains, the sanctuary and citadel of the primitive faith. That lamp is about to be extinguished at last, which has burned here during so many ages, and survived so many tempests. The mailed hand of the Pope is uplifted, and we wait to see the blow fall.

CHAPTER 4
Cataneo's Expedition (1488) Against the Dauphinese and Piedmontese

We see at this moment two armies on the march to attack the Christians inhabiting the Cottian and Dauphinese Alps. The sword now unsheathed is to be returned to its scabbard only when there breathes no longer in these mountains a single confessor of the faith condemned in the bull of Innocent VIII. The plan of the campaign was to attack at the same time on two opposite points of the great mountain-chain; and advancing, the one army from the south-east, and the other from the north-west, to meet in the Valley of Angrogna, the centre of the territory, and there strike the final blow. Let us follow first the French division of this host, that which is advancing against the Alps of Dauphine.

This portion of the crusaders was led by a daring and cruel man, skilled in such adventures, the Lord of La Palu. He ascended the mountains with his fanatics, and entered the Vale of Loyse, a deep gorge overhung by towering mountains. The inhabitants, seeing an armed force twenty times their own number enter their valley, despaired of being able to resist them, and prepared for flight. They placed their old people and children in rustic carts, together with their domestic utensils, and such store of victuals as the urgency of the occasion permitted them to collect, and driving their herds before them, they began to climb the rugged slopes of Mount Pelvoux, which rises some six thousand feet over the level of the valley. They sang canticles as they climbed the steeps, which served at once to smooth their rugged path, and to dispel their terrors. Not a few were overtaken and slaughtered, and theirs was perhaps the happier lot.

About half-way up there is an immense cavern, called Aigue-Froid, from the cold springs that gush out from its rocky walls. In front of the cavern is a platform of rock, where the spectator sees beneath him only fearful precipices, which must be clambered over before one can reach the entrance to the grotto. The roof of the cave forms a magnificent arch, which gradually subsides and contracts into a narrow passage, or threat, and then widens once more, and forms a roomy hall of irregular form. Into this grotto, as into an impregnable castle, did the Vaudois enter. Their women, infants, and old men, they placed in the inner hall; their cattle and sheep they distributed along the lateral cavities of the grotto. The able-bodied men posted themselves at the entrance. Having barricaded with huge stones both the doorway of the cave and the path that led to it, they deemed themselves secure. They had provisions to last, Cataneo says in his Memoirs, "two years;" and it would cost them little effort to hurl headlong down the precipices any one who should attempt to scale them in order to reach the entrance of the cavern.

But a device of their pursuer rendered all these precautions and defenses vain. La Palu ascended the mountain on the other side, and approaching the cave from above, let down his soldiers by ropes from the precipice overhanging the entrance to the grotto. The platform in front was thus secured by his soldiers. The Vaudois might have cut the ropes, and dispatched their foes as they were being lowered one by one, but the boldness of the maneuver would seem to have paralyzed them. They retreated into the cavern to find in it their grave. La Palu saw the danger of permitting his men to follow them into the depths of their hiding-place. He adopted the easier and safer method of piling up at its entrance all the wood he could collect and setting fire to it. A huge volume of black smoke began to roll into the cave, leaving to the unhappy inmates the miserable alternative of rushing out and falling by the sword that waited for them, or of remaining in the interior to be stifled by the murky vapor [Monstier, p. 128]. Some rushed out, and were massacred; but the greater part remained till death slowly approached them by suffocation. "When the cavern was afterwards examined," says Muston, "there were found in it 400 infants, suffocated in their cradles, or in the arms of their dead mothers. Altogether there perished in this cavern more than 3,000 Vaudois, including the entire population of Val Loyse. Cataneo distributed the property of these unfortunates among the vagabonds who accompanied him, and never again did the Vaudois Church raise its head in these blood-stained valleys" [Muston, p. 20].

The terrible stroke that fell on the Vale of Loyse was the shielding of the neighboring valleys of Argentiere and Fraissiniere. Their inhabitants had been destined to destruction also, but the fate of their co-religionists taught them that their only chance of safety lay in resistance. Accordingly, barricading the passes of their valleys, they showed such a front to the foe when he advanced, that he deemed it prudent to turn away and leave them in peace. This devastating tempest now swept along to discharge its violence on other valleys. "One would have thought," to use the words of Muston, "that the plague had passed along the track over which its march lay: it was on the inquisitors."

A detachment of the French army struck across the Alps in a south-east direction, holding their course toward the Waldensian Valleys, there to unite with the main body of the crusaders under Cataneo. They slaughtered, pillaged, and burned as they went onward, and at last arrived with dripping swords in the Valley of Pragelas.

The Valley of Pragelas, where we now see these assassins, sweeps along, from almost the summit of the Alps, to the south, watered by the rivers Clusone and Dora, and opens on the great plain of Piedmont, having Pinerolo on the one side and Susa on the other. It was then and long after under the dominion of France. "Prior to the revocation of the Edict of Nantes," says Muston, "the Vaudois of these valleys [that is, Pragelas, and the lateral vales branching out from it] possessed eleven parishes, eighteen churches, and sixty-four centers of religious assembling, where worship was celebrated morning and evening, in as many hamlets. It was in Laus, in Pragelas, that was held the famous synod where, 200 years before the Protestant Reformation, 140 Protestant pastors assembled, each accompanied by two or three lay deputies; and it was from the Val di Pragelas that the Gospel of God made its way into France prior to the fifteenth century" [Muston, part ii., p. 234].

This was the valley of Pragelas which had been the scene of the terrible tragedy of Christmas, 1400. Again terror, mourning, and death were carried into it. The peaceful inhabitants, who were expecting no such invasion, were busy reaping their harvests, when the horde of assassins burst upon them. In the first panic they abandoned their dwellings and fled. Many were overtaken and slain; hamlets and whole villages were given to the flames; nor could the caves in which multitudes sought refuge afford any protection. The horrible barbarity of the Val Loyse was repeated in the Valley of Pragelas. Combustible materials were piled up and fires kindled at the mouths of these hiding-places; and when extinguished, all was silent within. Folded together in one motionless heap lay mother and babe, patriarch and stripling; while the fatal smoke, which had cast them into that deep sleep, was eddying along the roof, and slowly making its exit into the clear sunlit summer sky. But the course of this destruction was stayed. After the first surprise the inhabitants took heart, and turning upon their murderers drove them from their valley, exacting a heavy penalty in the pursuit for the ravages they had committed in it.

We now turn to the Piedmontese portion of this army. It was led by the Papal legate, Cataneo, in person. It was destined to operate against those valleys in Piedmont which were the most ancient seat of these religionists, and were deemed the stronghold of the Vaudois heresy. Cataneo repaired to Pinerolo, which adjoins the frontier of the doomed territory. Thence he dispatched a band of preaching monks to convert the men of the Valleys. These missionaries returned without having, so far as appears made a single convert. The legate now put his soldiers in motion. Traversing the glorious plain, the Clusone gleaming out through rich corn-fields and vineyards on their left, and the mighty rampart of the hills, with their chestnut forests, their pasturages and snows, rising grandly on their right, and turning round the shoulder of the copse-clad Bricherasio, this army, with another army of pillagers and cut-throats in its rear, advanced up the long avenue that leads to La Torre, the capital of the Valleys, and sat down before it. They had come against a simple, unarmed people, who knew how to tend their vines, and lead their herds to pasture, but were ignorant of the art of war. It seemed as if the last hour of the Waldensian race had struck.

Seeing this mighty host before their Valleys, the Waldenses sent off two of their patriarchs to request an interview with Cataneo, and turn, if possible, his heart to peace. Jolin Campo and John Desiderio were dispatched on this embassy. "Do not condemn us without hearing us," said they, "for we are Christians and faithful subjects; and our Barbes are prepared to prove, in public or in private, that our doctrines are conformable to the Word of God ... Our hope in God is greater than our desire to please men; beware how you draw down upon yourselves His anger by persecuting us; for remember that, if God so wills it, all the forces you have assembled against us will nothing avail."

These were weighty words, and they were meekly spoken, but as to changing Cataneo's purpose, or softening the hearts of the ruffian-host which he led, they might as well have been addressed to the rocks which rose around the speakers. Nevertheless, they fell not to the ground.

Cataneo, believing that the Vaudois herdsmen would not stand an hour before his men-at-arms, and desirous of striking a finishing blow, divided his army into a number of attacking parties, which were to begin the battle on various points at the same time. The folly of extending his line so as to embrace the whole territory led to Cataneo's destruction; but his strategy was rewarded with a few small successes at first.

One troop was stationed at the entrance of the Val Lucerna; we shall follow its march till it disappears on the mountains which it hopes to conquer, and then we shall return and narrate the more decisive operations of the campaign under Cataneo in the Val Angrogna.

The first step of the invaders was to occupy the town of La Torre, situated on the angle formed by the junction of the Val Lucerna and the Val Angrogna, the silver Pelice at its feet and the shadow of the Castelluzzo covering it. The soldiers were probably spared the necessity or denied the pleasure of slaughter, the inhabitants having fled to the mountains. The valley beyond La Torre is too open to admit of being defended, and the troop advanced along it unopposed. Than this theatre of war nothing in ordinary times is more peaceful, nothing more grand. A carpet of rich meadows clothes it from side to side; fruitful trees fleck it with their shadows; the Pelice waters it; and on either hand is a wall of mountains, whose sides display successive zones of festooned vines, golden grain, dark chestnut forests, and rich pasturages. Over these are hung stupendous battlements of rock; and above all, towering high in air, are the everlasting peaks in their robes of ice and snow. But the sublimities of nature were nothing to men whose thoughts were only of blood.

43

Pursuing their march up the valley, the soldiers next came to Villaro. It is situated about midway between the entrance and head of Lucerna, on a ledge of turn in the side of the great mountains, raised some 200 feet above the Pelice, which flows past at about a quarter of a mile's distance. The troop had little difficulty in taking possession. Most of the inhabitants, warned of the approach of danger, had fled to the Alps. What Cataneo's troops inflicted on those who had been unable to make their escape, no history records. The half of Lucerna, with the towns of La Torre and Villaro and their hamlets, was in the occupation of Cataneo's soldiers; their march so far had been a victorious one, though certainly not a glorious one, such victories as they had gained being only over unarmed peasants and bed-rid women.

Resuming their march the troop came next to Bobbio. The name of Bobbio is not unknown in classic story. It nestles at the base of gigantic cliffs, where the lofty summit of the Col la Croix points the way to France, and overhangs a path which apostolic feet may have trodden. The Pelice is seen forging its way through the dark gorges of the mountains in a thundering torrent, and meandering in a flood of silver along the valley.

At this point the grandeur of the Val Lucerna attains its height. Let us pause to survey the scene that must here have met the eyes of Cataneo's soldiers, and which, one would suppose, might have turned them from their cruel purpose. Immediately behind Bobbio shoots up the "Barion," symmetrical as Egyptian obelisk, but far taller and more massive. Its summit rises 3,000 feet above the roof of the little town. Compared with this majestic monolith the proudest monument of Europe's proudest capital is a mere toy. Yet even the Barion is but one item in this assemblage of glories. Overtopping it behind, and sweeping round the extremity of the valley, is a glorious amphitheatre of crags and precipices, enclosed by a background of great mountains, some rounded like domes, others sharp as needles; and rising out of this sea of hills, are the grander and loftier forms of the Alp des Rousses and the Col de Malaure, which guard the gloomy pass that winds its way through splintered rocks and under overhanging precipices, till it opens into the valleys of the French Protestants, and lands the traveler on the plains of Dauphine. In this unrivalled amphitheatre sits Bobbio, in summer buried in blossoms and fruit, and in winter wrapped in the shadows of its great mountains, and the mists of their tempests. What a contrast between the still repose and grand sublimity of nature and the dreadful errand on which the men now pressing forward to the little town are bent! To them nature speaks in vain! they are engrossed with but one thought.

The capture of Bobbio-an easy task-put the soldiers in possession of the entire Valley of Lucerna; its inhabitants had been chased to the Alps, or their blood mingled with the waters of their own Pelice. Other and remoter expeditions were now projected. Their plan was to traverse the Col Julien, sweep down on the Valley of Prali, which lies on the north of it, chastise its inhabitants, pass on to the Valleys of San Martino and Perosa, and pursuing the circuit of the Valleys, and clearing the ground as they went onward of its inveterate heresy, at least of its heretics, join the main body of crusaders, who, they expected, would by this time have finished their work in the Valley of Angrogna, and all together celebrate their victory. They would then be able to say that they had gone the round of the Waldensian territory, and had at last effected the long-meditated work, so often attempted, but hitherto in vain, of the utter extirpation of its heresy. But the war was destined to have a very different termination.

The expedition across the Col Julien was immediately commenced. A corps of 700 men was detached from the army in Lucerna for this service [Monastier, p. 129]. The ascent of the mountain opens immediately on the north side of Bobbio. We see the soldiers toiling upwards on the track, which is a mere foot-path formed by the herdsmen. At every short distance they pass the thick-planted chalets and hamlets sweetly embowered amid mantling vines, or the branches of the apple and cherry tree, or the goodlier chestnut; but the inhabitants have fled. They have now reached a great height on the mountainside. Beneath is Bobbio, a speck of brown. There is the Valley of Lucerna, a ribbon of green, with a thread of silver woven into it, and lying along amid masses of mighty rocks. There, across Lucerna, are the great mountains that enclose the Valley of Rora, standing up in the silent sky; on the right are the spiky crags that bristle along the Pass of Miraboue, that leads to France, and yonder in the east is a glimpse of the far-extending Plains of Piedmont.

But the summit is yet a long way off, and the soldiers of the Papal legate, bearing their weapons, to be employed, not in venturesome battle, but in cowardly massacre, toil up the ascent. As they gain on the mountain, they look down on pinnacles which half an hour before had looked down on them. Other heights, tall as the former, still rise above them; they climb to these airy spires, which in their turn sink beneath their feet. This process they repeat again and again, and at last they come out upon the downs that clothe the shoulders of the mountain. Now it is that the scene around them becomes one of stupendous and inexpressible grandeur. Away to the east, now fully under the eye, is the plain of Piedmont, green as meadow, and level as ocean. At their feet yawn gorges and abysses, while spiky pinnacles peer up from below as if to buttress the mountain. The horizon is filled with Alpine peaks, conspicuous among which, on the east, is the Col la Vechera, whose snow-clad summit draws the eye to the more than classic valley over which it towers, where the Barbes in ancient days were wont to assemble in synod, and whence their missionaries went forth, at the peril of life, to distribute the Scriptures and sow the seed of the Kingdom. It was not unmarked, doubtless, by this corps, forming, as they meant it should do, the terminating point of their expedition in the Val di Angrogna. On the west, the crowning glory of the scene was Monte Viso, standing up in bold relief in the ebon vault, in a robe of silver. But in vain had Nature spread out her magnificence before men who had neither eyes to see nor hearts to feel her glory.

Climbing on their hands and knees the steep grassy slope in which the pass terminates, they looked down from the summit on the Valley of Prali, at that moment a scene of peace. Its great snow-clad hills, conspicuous among which is the Col d'Abries, kept guard around it. Down their sides rolled foaming torrents, which, uniting in the valley, flowed along in a full and rapid river. Over the bosom of the plain were scattered numerous hamlets. Suddenly on the mountains above had gathered this flock of vultures that with greedy eyes were looking down upon their prey. Impatient to begin their work, the 700 assassins rushed down on the plain.

The troop had reckoned that, no tidings of their approach having reached this secluded valley, they would fall upon its unarmed peasants as falls the avalanche, and crush them. But it was not to be so. Instead of fleeing, panic-struck, as the invaders expected, the men of Prali hastily assembled, and stood to their defense. Battle was joined at the hamlet of Pommiers. The weapons of the Vaudois were rude, but their trust in God, and their indignation at the cowardly and bloody assault, gave them strength and courage. The Piedmontese soldiers, wearied with the rugged, slippery tracks they had traversed, fell beneath the blows of their opponents. Every man of them was cut down with the exception of one ensign. Of all the 700, he alone survived. During the carnage, he made his escape, and ascending the banks of a mountain torrent, he crept into a cavity which the summer heats had formed in a mass of snow. There he remained hid for some days; at last, cold and hunger drove him forth to cast himself upon the mercy of the men of Prali. They were generous enough to pardon this solitary survivor of the host that had come to massacre them. They sent him back across the Col Julien, to tell those from whom he had come that the Vaudois had courage to fight for their hearths and altars, and that of the army of 700 which they had sent to slay them, he only had escaped to carry tidings of the fate which had befallen his companions.

CHAPTER 5
Failure of Cataneo's Expedition

T he camp of Cataneo was pitched almost at the gates of La Torre, beneath the shadow of the Castelluzzo. The Papal legate is about to try to force his way into the Val di Angrogna. This valley opens hard by the spot where the legate had established his camp, and runs on for a dozen miles into the Alps, a magnificent succession of narrow gorges and open dells, walled throughout by majestic mountains, and terminating in a noble circular basin-the Pra del Tor-which is set round with snowy peaks, and forms the most venerated spot in all the Waldensian territory, inasmuch as it was the seat of their college, and the meeting-place of their Barbes.

In the Pra del Tor, or Meadow of the Tower, Cataneo expected to surprise the mass of the Waldensian people, now gathered into it as being the strongest refuge which their hills afforded. There, too, he expected to be joined by the corps which he had sent round by Lucerna to make the circuit of the Valleys, and after devastating Prali and San Martino, to climb the mountain barrier and join their companions in the Pra, little imagining that the soldiers he had dispatched on that errand of massacre were now enriching with their corpses the Valleys they had been sent to subdue. In that same spot where the Barbes had so often met in synod, and enacted rules for the government of their Church and the spread of their faith, the Papal legate would reunite his victorious host, and finish the campaign by proclaiming that now the Waldensian heresy, root and branch, was extinct.

The Waldenses-their humble supplication for peace having been contemptuously rejected, as we have already said-had three courses in their choice-to go to mass, to be butchered as sheep, or to fight for their lives. They chose the last, and made ready for battle. But first they must remove to a place of safety all who were unable to bear arms.

Packing up their kneading-troughs, their ovens, and other culinary utensils, laying their aged on their shoulders, and their sick in couches, and leading their children by the hand, they began to climb the hills, in the direction of the Pra del Tor, at the head of the Val di Angrogna. Transporting their household stuff, they could be seen traversing the rugged paths, and making the mountains resound with psalms, which they sweetly sung as they journeyed up the ascent. Those who remained busied themselves in manufacturing pikes and other weapons of defense and attack, in repairing the barricades, in arranging themselves into fighting parties, and assigning to the various corps the posts they were to defend.

Cataneo now put his soldiers in motion. Advancing to near the town of La Torre, they made a sharp turn to the right, and entered the Val di Angrogna. Its opening offers no obstruction, being soft and even as any meadow in all England. By-and-by it begins to swell into the heights of Rocomaneot, where the Vaudois had resolved to make a stand. Their fighting men were posted along its ridge. Their army was of the simplest. The bow was almost their only weapon of attack. They wore bucklers of skin, covered with the bark of the chestnut-tree, the better to resist thrust of pike or cut of sword. In the hollow behind, protected by the rising ground on which their fathers, husbands, and brothers were posted, were a number of women and children, gathered there for shelter. The Piedmontese host pressed up the acclivity, discharging a shower of arrows as they advanced, and the Waldensian line on which these missiles fell, seemed to waver, and to be on the point of giving way. Those behind, espying the danger, fell on their knees and, extending their hands in supplication to the God of battles, cried aloud, "O God of our fathers, help us! O God, deliver us!" That cry was heard by the attacking host, and especially by one of its captains, Le Noir of Mondovi, or the Black Mondovi, a proud, bigoted, bloodthirsty man. He instantly shouted out that his soldiers would give the answer, accompanying his threat with horrible blasphemies. The Black Mondovi raised his visor as he spoke. At the instant an arrow from the bow of Pierre Revel, of Angrogna, entering between his eyes, transfixed his skull, and he fell on the earth a corpse.

The fall of this daring leader disheartened the Papal army. The soldiers began to fall back. They were chased down the slopes by the Vaudois, who now descended upon them like one of their own mountain torrents. Having driven their invaders to the plain, cutting off not a few in their flight, they returned as the evening began to fall, to celebrate with songs, on the heights where they had won it, the victory with which it had pleased the God of their fathers to crown their arms.

Cataneo burned with rage and shame at being defeated by these herdsmen. In a few days, reassembling his host, he made a second attempt to enter the Angrogna. This promised to be successful. He passed the height of Rocomaneot, where he had encountered his first defeat, without meeting any resistance. He led his soldiers into the narrow defiles beyond. Here great rocks overhang the path: mighty chestnut-trees fling their branches across the way, veiling it in gloom, and far down thunders the torrent that waters the valley. Still advancing, he found himself, without fighting, in possession of the ample and fruitful expanse into which, these defiles passed, the valley opens. He was now master so far of the Val di Angrogna, comprehending the numerous hamlets, with their finely cultivated fields and vineyards, on the left of the torrent. But he had seen none of its inhabitants. These, he knew, were with the men of Lucerna in the Pra del Tor. Between him and his prey rose the "Barricade," a steep unscaleable mountain, which runs like a wall across the valley, and forms a rampart to the famous "Meadow," which combines the solemnity of sanctuary with the strength of citadel.

Must the advance of the Papal legate and his army here end? It seemed as if it must. Cataneo was in a vast cul-de-sac. He could see the white peaks round the Pra, but between him and the Pra itself rose, in Cyclopean strength and height, the Barricade. He searched and, unhappily for himself, found an entrance. Some convulsion of nature has here rent the mountains, and through the long, narrow, and dark chasm thus formed lies the one only path that leads to the head of Angrogna. The leader of the Papal host boldly ordered his men to enter and traverse this frightful gorge, not knowing how few of them he should ever lead back. The only pathway through this chasm is a rocky ledge on the side of the mountains, so narrow that not more than two abreast can advance along it. If assailed either in front, or in rear, or from above, there is absolutely no retreat. Nor is there room for the party attacked to fight. The pathway is hung midway between the bottom of the gorge, along which rolls the stream, and the summit of the mountain. Here the naked cliff runs sheer up for at least one thousand feet; there it leans over the path in stupendous masses, which look as if about to fall. Here lateral fissures admit the golden beams of the sun, which relieve the darkness of the pass, and make it visible. There a half-acre or so of level space gives standing-room on the mountain's side to a clump of birches, with their tall silvery trunks, or a chalet, with its bit of bright close-shaven meadow. But these only partially relieve the terrors of the chasm, which runs on from one to two miles, when, with a burst of light, and a sudden flashing of white peaks on the eye, it opens into an amphitheatre of meadow of dimensions so goodly, that an entire nation might find room to encamp in it.

It was into this terrible defile that the soldiers of the Papal legate now marched. They kept advancing, as best they could, along the narrow ledge. They were now nearing the Pra. It seemed impossible for their prey to escape them. Assembled on this spot the Waldensian people had but one neck, and the Papal soldiers, so Cataneo believed, were to sever that neck at a blow. But God was watching over the Vaudois. He had said of the Papal legate and his army, as of another tyrant of former days, "I will put my hook in thy nose, and my bridle in thy lips, and I will cause thee to return by the way by which thou camest." But by what agency was the advance of that host to be stayed? Will some mighty angel smite Cataneo's army, as he did Sennacherib's? No angel blockaded the pass. Will thunder-bolts and hailstones be rained upon Cataneo's soldiers, as of old on Sisera's? The thunders slept; the hail fell not. Will earthquake and whirlwind discomfit them? No earthquake rocked the ground; no whirlwinds rent the mountains. The instrumentality now put in motion to shield the Vaudois from destruction was one of the lightest and frailest in all nature; yet no bars of adamant could have more effectually shut the pass, and brought the march of the host to an instant halt.

A white cloud, no bigger than a man's hand, unobserved by the Piedmontese, but keenly watched by the Vaudois, was seen to gather on the mountain's summit, about the time the army would be entering the defile. That cloud grew rapidly bigger and blacker. It began to descend. It came rolling down the mountain's side, wave on wave, like an ocean tumbling out of heaven-a sea of murky vapor. It fell right into the chasm in which was the Papal army, sealing it up, and filling it from top to bottom with a thick black fog. In a moment the host were in night; they were bewildered, stupefied, and could see neither before nor behind, could neither advance nor retreat. They halted in a state bordering on terror [Monastier, pp. 133-4].

The Waldenses interpreted this as an interposition of Providence in their behalf. It had given them the power of repelling the invader. Climbing the slopes of the Pra, and issuing from all their hiding-places in its environs, they spread themselves over the mountains, the paths of which were familiar to them, and while the host stood riveted beneath them, caught in the double toils of the defile and the mist, they tore up huge stones and rocks, and sent them thundering down into the ravine. The Papal soldiers were crushed where they stood. Nor was this all. Some of the Waldenses boldly entered the chasm, sword in hand, and attacked them in front. Consternation seized the Piedmontese host. panic impelled them to flee, but their effort to escape was more fatal than the sword of the Vaudois, or the rocks that, swift as arrow, came bounding down the mountain. They jostled one another; they threw each other down in the struggle; some were trodden to death; others were rolled over the precipice, and crushed on the rocks below, or drowned in the torrent, and so perished miserably [Monastier, p. 134].

The fate of one of these invaders has been preserved in story. He was a certain Captain Saquet, a man, it is said, of gigantic stature, from Polonghera, in Piedmont. He began, like his Philistine prototype, to vent curses on the Waldensian dogs. The words were yet in his mouth when his foot slipped. Rolling over the precipice, and tumbling into the torrent of the Angrogna, he was carried away by the stream, and his body finally deposited in a deep eddy or whirlpool, called in the patois of the country a "tompie," from the noise made by its waters. It bears to this day the name of the Tompie do Saquet, or Gulf of Saquet.

[The Author was shown this pool when he visited the chasm. None of the Waldensian valleys is better illustrated by the sad, yet glorious, scenes of their martyrdom than this Valley of Angrogna. Every rock in it has its story. As you pass through it you are shown the spot where young children were dashed against the stones-the spot where men and women, stripped naked, were rolled up as balls, and precipitated down the mountain, and where, caught by the stump of tree, or projecting angle of rock, they hung transfixed, enduring for days the agony of a living death. You are shown the entrance of caves, into which some hundreds of the Vaudois having fled, their enemies, lighting a fire at the mouth of their hiding place, ruthlessly killed them all. Time would fail to tell even a tithe of what has been done and suffered in this famous pass.]

This war hung above the Valleys, like a cloud of tempest, for a whole year. It inflicted much suffering and loss upon the Waldenses; their homes were burned, their fields devastated, their goods carried off, and their persons slain; but the invaders suffered heavier losses than they inflicted. Of the 18,000 regular troops, to which we may add about an equal number of desperadoes, with which the campaign opened, few ever returned to their homes. They left their bones on the mountains they had come to subdue. They were cut off mostly in detail. They were led weary chases from valley to mountain and from mountain to valley. The rocks rolled upon them gave them at once death and burial. They were met in narrow defiles and cut to pieces. Flying parties of Waldenses would suddenly issue from the mist, or from some cave known only to themselves, attack and discomfit the foe, and then as suddenly retreat into the friendly vapor or the sheltering rock. Thus it came to pass that, in the words of Muston, "this army of invaders vanished from the Vaudois mountains as rain in the sands of the desert" [Muston, p. 11].

"God," says Leger, "turned the heart of their prince toward this poor people." He sent a prelate to their Valleys, to assure them of his good-will, and to intimate his wish to receive their deputies. They sent twelve of their more venerable men to Turin, who being admitted into the duke's presence, gave him such an account of their faith, that he candidly confessed that he had been misled in what he had done against them, and would not again suffer such wrongs to be inflicted upon them. He several times said that he "had not so virtuous, so faithful, and so obedient subjects as the Vaudois" [Leger, livr. ii., p. 26].

He caused the deputies a little surprise by expressing a wish to see some of the Vaudois children. Twelve infants, with their mothers, were straightway sent for from the valley of Angrogna, and presented before the prince. He examined them narrowly. He found them well formed, and testified his admiration of their healthy faces, clear eyes and lively prattle. He had been told, he said, that "the Vaudois children were monsters, with only one eye placed in the middle of the forehead, four rows of black teeth, and other similar deformities" [Ibid.].

The prince, Charles II, a youth of only twenty years, but humane and wise, confirmed the privileges and immunities of the Vaudois, and dismissed them with his promise that they should be unmolested in the future.[1] The Churches of the Valleys now enjoyed a short respite from persecution.

ENDNOTES

[1] Leger and Gilles say that it was Philip VII who put an end to this war. Monastier says they "are mistaken, for this prince was then in France, and did not begin to reign till 1496." This peace was granted in 1489.

CHAPTER 6
Synod in the Waldensian Valleys

The Duke of Savoy was sincere in the promise that the Vaudois should not be disturbed, but fully to make it good was not altogether in his power. He could take care that such armies of crusaders as that which mustered under the standard of Cataneo should not invade their Valleys, but he could not guard them from the secret machinations of the priesthood. In the absence of the armed crusader, the missionary and the inquisitor assailed them. Some were seduced, others were kidnapped, and carried off to the Holy Office. To these annoyances was added the yet greater evil of a decaying piety. A desire for repose made many conform outwardly to the Romish Church. "In order to be shielded from all interruption in their journeys on business, they obtained from the priests, who were settled in the Valleys, certificates or testimonials of their being Papists" [Monastier, Hist. of the Vaudois, p. 138]. To obtain this credential it was necessary to attend the Romish chapel, to confess, to go to mass, and to have their children baptized by the priests. For this shameful and criminal dissimulation they fancied they made amends by muttering to themselves when they entered the Romish temples, "Cave of robbers, may God confound thee!" [Monastier, Hist. of the Vaudois, p. 138]. At the same time they continued to attend the preaching of the Vaudois pastors, and to submit themselves to their censures. But beyond all question the men who practiced these deceits, and the Church that tolerated them, had greatly declined. That old vine seemed to be dying. A little while and it would disappear from off those mountains which it had so long covered with the shadow of its boughs.

But He who had planted it "looked down from heaven and visited it." It was now that the Reformation broke out. The river of the Water of Life was opened a second time, and began to flow through Christendom. The old and dying stock in the Alps, drinking of the celestial stream, lived anew; its boughs began to be covered with blossoms and fruit as of old.

The Reformation had begun its career, and had already stirred most of the countries of Europe to their depths before tidings of the mighty change reached these secluded mountains. When at last the great news was announced, the Vaudois "were as men who dreamed." Eager to have them confirmed, and to know to what extent the yoke of Rome had been cast off by the nations of Europe, they sent forth Pastor Martin, of the valley of Lucerna, on a mission of inquiry. In 1526 he returned with the amazing intelligence that the light of the old Evangel had broken on Germany, on Switzerland, on France, and that every day was adding to the number of those who openly professed the same doctrines to which the Vaudois had borne witness from ancient times. To attest what he said, he produced the books he had received in Germany containing the views of the Reformers [Gilles, p. 30. Monastier, p. 141].

The remnant of the Vaudois on the north of the Alps also sent out men to collect information respecting that great spiritual revolution which had so surprised and gladdened them. In 1530 the Churches of Provence and Dauphine commissioned George Morel, of Merindol, and Pierre Masson, of Burgundy, to visit the Reformers of Switzerland and Germany, and bring them word touching their doctrine and manner of life. The deputies met in conference with the members of the Protestant Churches of Neuchatel, Morat, and Bern. They had also interviews with Berthold Haller and William Farel. Going on to Basle they presented to OEcolampadius, in October, 1530, a document in Latin, containing a complete account of their ecclesiastical discipline, worship, doctrine, and manners. They begged in return that EOcolampadius would say whether he approved of the order and doctrine of their Church, and if he held it to be defective, to specify in what points, and to what extent. The elder Church submitted itself to the younger.

The visit of these two pastors of this ancient Church gave unspeakable joy to the Reformer of Basle. He heard in them the voice of the primitive and apostolic

Church speaking to the Christians of the sixteenth century, and bidding them welcome within the gates of the City of God. What a miracle was before him! For ages had this Church been in the fires, yet she had not been consumed. Was not this encouragement to those who were just entering into persecutions not less terrific? "We render thanks," said OEcolampadius in his letter, October 13th, 1530, to the Churches of Provence, "to our most gracious Father that he has called you into such marvelous light, during ages in which such thick darkness has covered almost the whole world under the empire of Antichrist. We love you as brethren."

But his affection for them did not blind him to their declensions, nor make him withhold those admonitions which he saw to be needed. "As we approve of many things among you," he wrote, "so there are several which we wish to see amended. We are informed that the fear of persecution has caused you to dissemble and to conceal your faith ... There is no concord between Christ and Belial. You commune with unbelievers; you take part in their abominable masses, in which the death and passion of Christ are blasphemed. ... I know your weakness, but it becomes those who have been redeemed by the blood of Christ to be more courageous. It is better for us to die than to be overcome by temptation." It was thus that OEcolampadius, speaking in the name of the Church of the Reformation, repaid the Church of the Alps for the services she had rendered to the world in former ages. By sharp, faithful, brotherly rebuke, he sought to restore to her the purity and glory which she had lost.

Having finished with OEcolampadius, the deputies went on to Strasburg. There they had interviews with Bucer and Capito. A similar statement of their faith to the Reformers of that city drew forth similar congratulations and counsels. In the clear light of her morning the Reformation Church saw many things which had grown dim in the evening of the Vaudois Church; and the Reformers willingly permitted their elder sister the benefit of their own wider views. If the men of the sixteenth century recognized the voice of primitive Christianity speaking in the Vaudois, the latter heard the voice of the Bible, or rather of God himself, speaking in the Reformers, and submitted themselves with modesty and docility to their reproofs. The last had become first.

A manifold interest belongs to the meeting of these two Churches. Each is a miracle to the other. The preservation of the Vaudois Church for so many ages, amid the fires of persecution, made her a wonder to the Church of the sixteenth century. The bringing up of the latter from the dead made her a yet greater wonder to the Church of the first century. These two Churches compare their respective beliefs: they find that their creeds are not twain, but one. They compare the sources of their knowledge: they find that they have both of them drawn their doctrine from the Word of God; they are not two Churches, they are one. They are the elder and younger members of the same glorious family, the children of the same Father. What a magnificent monument of the true antiquity and genuine catholicity of Protestantism!

Only one of the two Provence deputies returned from their visit to the Reformers of Switzerland. On their way back, at Dijon, suspicion, from some cause or other, fell on Pierre Masson. He was thrown into prison, and ultimately condemned and burned. His fellow-deputy was allowed to go on his way. George Morel, bearing the answers of the Reformers, and especially the letters of OEcolampadius, happily arrived in safety in Provence.

The documents he brought with him were much canvassed. Their contents caused these two ancient Churches mingled joy and sorrow; the former, however, greatly predominating. The news touching the numerous body of Christians, now appearing in many lands, so full of knowledge, and faith, and courage, was literally astounding. The confessors of the Alps thought that they were alone in the world; every successive century saw their numbers thinning, and their spirit growing less resolute; their ancient enemy, on the other hand, was steadfastly widening her dominion and strengthening her sway. A little longer, they imagined, and all public faithful profession of the Gospel would cease. It was at that moment they were told that a new army of champions had arisen to maintain the old battle. This announcement explained and justified the past to them, for now they beheld the fruits of their fathers' blood. They who had fought the battle were not to have the honor of the victory. That was reserved for combatants who had newly come into the field. They had forfeited this reward, they painfully felt, by their defections; hence the regret that mingled with their joy.

They proceeded to discuss the answers that should be made to the Churches of the Protestant faith, considering especially whether they should adopt the reforms urged upon them in the communications which their deputies had brought back from the Swiss and German Reformers. The great majority of the Vaudois barbes were of opinion that they ought. A small minority, however, were opposed to this, because they thought that it did not become the new disciples to dictate to the old, or because they themselves were secretly inclined to the Roman superstitions. They went back again to the Reformers for advice; and, after repeated interchange of views, it was finally resolved to convene a synod in the Valleys, at which all the questions between the two Churches might be debated, and the relations which they were to sustain towards each other in time to come, determined. If the Church of the Alps was to continue apart, as before the Reformation, she felt that she must justify her position by proving the existence of great and substantial differences in doctrine between herself and the newly-arisen Church. But if no such differences existed, she would not, and dared not, remain separate and alone; she must unite with the Church of the Reformation.

It was resolved that the coming synod should be a truly ecumenical one-a general assembly of all the children of the Protestant faith. A hearty invitation was sent forth, and it was cordially and generally responded to. All the Waldensian Churches in the bosom of the Alps were represented in this synod. The Albigensian communities on the north of the chain, and the Vaudois Churches in Calabria, sent deputies to it. The Churches of French Switzerland chose William Farel and Anthony Saunier to attend it [Ruchat, tom. iii., pp. 176,557.] From even more distant lands, as Bohemia, came men to deliberate and vote in this famous convention.

The representatives assembled on the 12th of October, 1532. Two years earlier the Augsburg Confession had been given to the world, marking the culmination of the German Reformation. A year before, Zwingli had died on the field of Cappel. In France, the Reformation was beginning to be illustrated by the heroic deaths of its children. Calvin had not taken his prominent place at Geneva, but he was already enrolled under the Protestant banner. The princes of the Schmalkald League were standing at bay in the presence of Charles V. It was a critical yet glorious era in the annals of Protestantism which saw this assembly convened. It met at the town of

Chamforans, in the heart of the Valley of Angrogna. There are few grander or stronger positions in all that valley than the site occupied by this little town. The approach to it was defended by the heights of Rocomaneot and La Serre, and by defiles which now contract, now widen, but are everywhere overhung by great rocks and mighty chestnut trees, behind and above which rise the taller peaks, some of them snow-clad. A little beyond La Serre is the plateau on which the town stood, overlooking the grassy bosom of the valley, which is watered by the crystal torrent, dotted by numerous chalets, and runs on for about two miles, till shut in by the steep, naked precipices of the Barricade, which, stretching from side to side of Angrogna, leaves only the long, dark chasm we have already described, as the pathway to the Pra del Tor, whose majestic mountains here rise on the sight and suggest to the traveler the idea that he is drawing nigh some city of celestial magnificence. The town of Chamforans does not now exist; its only representative at this day is a solitary farmhouse.

The synod sat for six consecutive days. All the points raised in the communications received from the Protestant Churches were freely discussed by the assembled barbes and elders. Their findings were embodied in a "Short Confession of Faith," which Monastier says "may be considered as a supplement to the ancient Confession of Faith of the year 1120, which it does not contradict in any point" [Hist. of the Vaud., p. 146.] It consists of seventeen articles," the chief of which are the Moral inability of man; election to eternal life; the will of God, as made known in the Bible, the only rule of duty; and the doctrine of two Sacraments only, Baptism and the Lord's Supper. [It is entitled, says Leger, "A Brief Confession of Faith made by the Pastors and Heads of the Families of the Valleys of Piedmont." "It is preserved," he adds, "with other documents in the Library of the University of Cambridge." (Hist. des Vaud., livr. i., p. 95.)]

The lamp which had been on the point of expiring began, after this synod, to burn with its former brightness. The ancient spirit of the Waldenses revived. They no longer practiced these dissimulations and cowardly concealments to which they had had recourse to avoid persecution. They no longer feared to confess their faith. Henceforward they were never seen at mass, or in the Popish churches. They refused to recognize the priests of Rome as ministers of Christ, and under no circumstances would they receive any spiritual benefit or service at their hands.

Another sign of the new life that now animated the Vaudois was their setting about the work of rebuilding their churches. For fifty years before, public worship may be said to have ceased in their Valleys. Their churches had been razed by the persecutor, and the Vaudois feared to rebuild them lest they should draw down upon themselves a new storm of violence and blood. A cave would serve at times as a place of meeting. In more peaceful years the house of their barbe, or of some of their chief men, would be converted into a church; and when the weather was fine, they would assemble on the mountain side, under the great boughs of their ancestral trees. But their old sanctuaries they dared not raise from the ruins into which the persecutor had cast them. They might say with the ancient Jews, "The holy and beautiful house in which our fathers praised Thee is burned with fire, and all our pleasant things are laid waste." but now, strengthened by the fellowship and counsels of their Protestant brethren, churches arose, and the worship of God was reinstituted. Hard by the place where the synod met, at Lorenzo, namely, was the first of these post-Reformation churches set up; others speedily followed in the other valleys; pastors were multiplied; crowds flocked to their preaching, and not a few came from the plains of Piedmont, and from remote parts of their valleys, to drink of these living waters again flowing in their land.

Yet another token did this old Church give of the vigorous life that was now flowing in her veins. This was a translation of the Scriptures into the French tongue. At the synod, the resolution was taken to translate and print both the Old and New Testaments, and, as this was to be done at the sole charge of the Vaudois, it was considered as their gift to the Churches of the Reformation. A most appropriate and noble gift! That Book which the Waldenses had received from the primitive Church-which their fathers had preserved with their blood-which their barbes had laboriously transcribed and circulated-they now put into the hands of the Reformers, constituting them along with themselves the custodians of this, the ark of the world's hopes. Robert Olivetan, a near relative of Calvin, was asked to undertake the translation, and he executed it with the help of his great kinsman, it is believed. It was printed in folio, in black letter, at Neuchatel, in the year 1535, by Pierre de Wingle, commonly called Picard. The entire expense was defrayed by the

Waldenses, who collected for this object 1,500 crowns of gold, a large sum for so poor a people. Thus did the Waldensian Church emphatically proclaim, at the commencement of this new era in her existence, that the Word of God was her one sole foundation.

As has been already mentioned, a commission to attend the synod had been given by the Churches of French Switzerland to Farel and Saunier. Its fulfillment necessarily involved great toil and peril. One crosses the Alps at this day so easily, that it is difficult to conceive the toil and danger that attended the journey then. The deputies could not take the ordinary tracks across the mountains for fear of pursuit; they were compelled to travel by unfrequented paths. The way often led by the edge of precipices and abysses, up steep and dangerous ascents, and across fields of frozen snow. Nor were their pursuers the only dangers they had to fear; they were exposed to death from the blinding drifts and tempests of the hills. Nevertheless, they arrived in safety in the Valleys, and added by their presence and their counsels to the dignity of this the first great ecclesiastical assembly of modern times. Of this we have a somewhat remarkable proof. Three years thereafter, a Vaudois, Jean Peyrel, of Angrogna, being cast into prison, deposed on his trial that "he had kept guard for the ministers who taught the good law, who were assembled in the town of Chamforans, in the centre of Angrogna; and that amongst others present there was one called Farel, who had a red beard, and a beautiful white horse; and two others accompanied him, one of whom had a horse, almost black, and the other was very tall, and rather lame" [Gilles, p. 40. Monastier, p. 146].

CHAPTER 7

Persecutions and Martyrdoms

The Church of the Alps had peace for twenty-eight years. This was a time of great spiritual prosperity. Sanctuaries arose in all her Valleys; her pastors and teachers were found too few, and men of learning and zeal, some of them from foreign lands, pressed into her service. Individuals and families in the cities on the plain of Piedmont embraced her faith; and the crowds that attended her worship were continually growing. [George Morel states, in his Memoirs, that at this time there were more then 800,000 persons of the religion of the Vaudois. (Leger, Hist. des Vaudois, livr. ii., p. 27.) He includes, of course, in this estimate the Vaudois in the Valleys, on the plain of Piedmont, in Naples and Calabria, in the South of France, and in the countries of Germany.] In short, this venerable Church had a second youth. Her lamp, retrimmed, burned with a brightness that justified her time-honored motto, "A light shining in darkness." The darkness was not now so deep as it had been; the hours of night were drawing to a close. Nor was the Vaudois community the only light that now shone in Christendom. It was one of a constellation of lights, whose brilliance was beginning to irradiate the skies of the Church with an effulgence which no former age had known.

The exemption from persecution, which the Waldenses enjoyed during this period, was not absolute, but comparative. The lukewarm are seldom molested; and the quickened zeal of the Vaudois brought with it a revival of the persecutor's malignity, though it did not find vent in violences so dreadful as the tempests that had lately smitten them. Only two years after the synod-that is, in 1534--wholesale destruction fell upon the Vaudois Churches of Provence; but the sad story of their extinction will more appropriately be told elsewhere. In the valleys of Piedmont events were from time to time occurring that showed that the inquisitor's vengeance had been scotched, not killed. While the Vaudois as a race were prosperous, their churches multiplying, and their faith extending its geographical area from one year to another, individual Vaudois were being at times seized, and put to death, at the stake, on the rack, or by the cord.

Three years after, the persecution broke out anew, and raged for a short time. Charles III of Savoy, a prince of mild manners, but under the rule of the priests, being solicited by the Archbishop of Turin and the inquisitor of the same city, gave his consent to "hunting down" the heretics of the Valleys. The commission was given to a nobleman of the name of Bersour, whose residence was at Pinerolo, near the entrance of the Valley of Perosa. Bersour, a man of savage disposition, collected a troop of 500 horse and foot, and attacked the Valley of Angrogna. He was repulsed, but the storm which had rolled away from the mountains fell upon the plains. Turning to the Vaudois who resided around his own residence, he seized a great number of persons, whom he threw into the prisons and convents of Pinerolo and the Inquisition of Turin. Many of them suffered in the flames. One of these martyrs, Catalan Girard, quaintly taught the spectators a parabolic lesson, standing at the pile. From amid the flames he asked for two stones, which were instantly brought him. The crowd looked on in silence, curious to know what he meant to do with them. Rubbing them against each other, he said, "You think to extinguish our poor Churches by your persecutions. You can no more do so, than I with my feeble hands can crush these stones" [Leger, livr. ii., p. 27].

Heavier tempests seemed about to descend, when suddenly the sky cleared above the confessors of the Alps. It was a change in the politics of Europe in this instance, as in many others, that stayed the arm of persecution. Francis I of France demanded of Charles, Duke of Savoy, permission to march an army through his dominions. The object of the French king was the recovery of the Duchy of Milan, a long-contested prize between himself and Charles V. The Duke of Savoy refused the request of his brother monarch; but reflecting that the passes of the Alps were in the hands of the men whom he was persecuting, and that should he continue his oppressions, the Vaudois might open the gates of his kingdom to the enemy, he sent orders to Bersour to stop the persecution in the Valleys.

In 1536, the Waldensian Church had to mourn the loss of one of the more distinguished of her pastors. Martin Gonin, of Angrogna-a man of public spirit and rare gifts-who had gone to Geneva on ecclesiastical affairs, was returning through Dauphine, when he was apprehended on suspicion of being a spy. He cleared himself of that charge, but the gaoler searching his person, and discovering certain papers upon him, he was convicted of what the parliament of Grenoble accounted a much greater crime-heresy. Condemned to die, he was led forth at night, and drowned in the river Isere. He would have suffered at the stake had not his persecutors feared the effect of his dying words upon the spectators [Monastier, p. 153].

There were others, also called to ascend the martyr-pile, whose names we must not pass over in silence. Two pastors returning from Geneva to their flocks in the Valleys, in company of three French Protestants, were seized at the Col de Tamiers, in Savoy, and carried to Chambery. There all five were tried, condemned, and burned. The fate of Nicolas Sartoire is yet more touching. He was a student of theology at Geneva, and held one of those bursaries which the Lords of Bern had allotted for the training of young men as pastors in the Churches of the Valleys. He set out to spend his holiday with his family in Piedmont. We know how Vaudois heart yearns for its native mountains; nor would the coming of the youth awaken less lively anticipations on the part of his friends. The paternal threshold, alas! he was never to cross; his native Valleys he was to tread no more. Traveling by the pass of St. Bernard, and the grand valley of Aosta, he had just passed the Italian frontier, when he was apprehended on the suspicion of heresy. It was the month of May, when all was life and beauty in the vales and mountains around him; he himself was in the spring-time of existence; it was hard to lay down life at such a moment; but the great captain from whose feet he had just come, had taught him that the first duty of a soldier of Christ is obedience. He confessed his Lord, nor could promises or threats-and both were tried-make him waver. He continued steadfast unto the end, and on the 4th of May, 1557, he was brought forth from his dungeon at Aosta, and burned alive [Leger, livr. ii., p. 29].

The martyr who died thus heroically at Aosta was a youth, the one we are now to contemplate was a man of fifty. Geofroi Varaile was a native of the town of Busco, in Piedmont. His father had been a captain in that army of murderers who, in 1488, ravaged the Valleys of Lucerna and Angrogna. The son in 1520 became a monk, and possessing the gift of a rare eloquence, he was sent on a preaching tour, in company with another cowled ecclesiastic, yet more famous, Bernardo Ochino of Sienna, the founder of the order of the Capuchins. The arguments of the men he was sent to convert staggered Varaile. He fled to Geneva, and in the city of the Reformers he was taught more fully the "way of life." Ordained as a pastor, he returned to the Valleys, where "like another Paul, says Leger, "he preached the faith he once destroyed." After a ministry of some months, he set out to pay a visit of a few days to his native town of Busco. He was apprehended by the monks who were lying in wait for him. He was condemned to death by the Inquisition of Turin. His execution took place in the castle-piazza of the same city, March 29th, 1558. He walked to the place where he was to die with a firm step and a serene countenance; he addressed the vast multitude around his pile in a way that drew tears from many eyes; after this, he began to sing with a loud voice, and so continued till he sank amid the flames [Leger, livr. ii., p. 29].

Two years before this, the same piazza, the castle-yard at Turin, had witnessed a similar spectacle. Barthelemy Hector was a bookseller in Poictiers. A man of warm but well-tempered zeal, he traveled as far as the Valleys, diffusing that knowledge that maketh wise unto salvation. In the assemblage of white peaks that look down on the Pra del Tor is one named La Vechera, so called because the cows love the rich grass that clothes its sides in summer-time. Barthelemy Hector would take his seat on the slopes of the mountain, and gathering the herdsmen and agriculturists of the Pra round him, would induce them to buy his books, by reading passages to them. Portions of the Scriptures also would he recite to the granddames and maidens as they watched their goats, or plied the distaff. His steps were tracked by the inquisitor, even amid these wild solitudes. He was dragged to Turin, to answer for the crime of selling Genevese books. His defense before his judges discovered an admirable courage and wisdom.

"You have been caught in the act," said his judge, "of selling books that contain heresy. What say you?"

"If the Bible is heresy to you, it is truth to me," replied the prisoner.

"But you use the Bible to deter men from going to mass," urged the judge.

"If the Bible deters men from going to mass," responded Barthelemy, "it is a proof that God disapproves of it, and that mass is idolatry."

The judge, deeming it expedient to make short shrift with such a heretic, exclaimed, "Retract."

"I have spoken only truth," said the bookseller, "can I change truth as I would a garment?"

His judges kept him some months in prison, in the hope that his recantation would save them the necessity of burning him. This unwillingness to have resort to the last penalty was owing to no feeling of pity for the prisoner, but entirely to the conviction that these repeated executions were endangering the cause of their Church. "The smoke of these martyr-piles," as was said with reference to the death of Patrick Hamilton, "was infecting those on whom it blew." But the constancy of Barthelemy compelled his persecutors to disregard these prudential considerations. At last, despairing of his abjuration, they brought him forth and consigned him to the flames. His behavior at the stake "drew rivers of tears," says Leger, "from the eyes of many in the Popish crowd around his stake, while others vented reproaches and invectives against the cruelty of the monks and the inquisitors [Leger, Livr. ii., p. 28].

These are only a few of the many martyrs by whom, even during this period of comparative peace and prosperity, the Church of the Valleys was called to testify against Rome. Some of these martyrs perished by cruel, barbarous, and most horrible methods. To recite all these cases would be beyond our purpose, and to depict the revolting and infamous details would be to narrate what no reader could peruse. We shall quote only part of the brief summary of Muston. "There is no town in Piedmont," says he, "under a Vaudois pastor, where some of our brethren have not been put to death ... Hugo Chiamps of Finestrelle had his entrails torn from his living body, at Turin. Peter Geymarali of Bobbio, in like manner, had his entrails taken out at Lucerna, and a fierce cat thrust in their place to torture him further; Maria Romano was buried alive at Rocco-patia; Magdalen Foulano underwent the same fate at San Giovanni; Susan Michelini was bound hand and foot, and left to perish of cold and hunger at Saracena. Bartholomew Fache, gashed with sabers, had the wounds filled up with quicklime, and perished thus in agony at Fenile; Daniel Michelini had his tongue torn out at Bobbio for having praised God. James Baridari perished covered with sulphurous matches, which had been forced into his flesh under the nails, between the fingers, in the nostrils, in the lips, and over all his body, and then lighted. Daniel Revelli had his mouth filled with gunpowder, which, being lighted, blew his head to pieces. Maria Monnen, taken at Liousa, had the flesh cut from her cheek and chin bone, so that her jaw was left bare, and she was thus left to perish. Paul Garnier was slowly sliced to pieces at Rora. Thomas Margueti was mutilated in an indescribable manner at Miraboco, and Susan Jaquin cut in bits at La Torre. Sara Rostagnol was slit open from the legs to the bosom, and so left to perish on the road between Eyral and Lucerna. Anne Charbonnier was impaled and carried thus on a pike, as a standard, from San Giovanni to La Torre. Daniel Rambaud, at Paesano, had his nails torn off, then his fingers chopped off, then his feet and his hands, then his arms and his legs, with each successive refusal on his part to abjure the Gospel" [Muston, Israel of the Alps, chap. 8.] Thus the roll of martyrs runs on, and with each new sufferer comes a new, a more excruciating and more horrible mode of torture and death.

We have already mentioned the demand which the King of France made upon the Duke of Savoy, Charles III, that he would permit him to march an army through his territories. The reply was a refusal; but Francis I must needs have a road into Italy. Accordingly he seized upon Piedmont, and held possession of it, together with the Waldensian valleys, for twenty-three years. The Waldenses had found the sway of Francis I more tolerant than that of their own princes; for though Francis hated Lutheranism, the necessities of his policy often compelled him to court the Lutherans, and so it came to pass that while he was burning heretics in Paris he spared them in the Valleys. But the general peace of Chateau Cambresis, April 3rd, 1559, restored Piedmont, with the exception of Turin, to its former rulers of the House of Savoy [Leger, livr. ii., p. 29.] Charles III had been succeeded in 1553 by Emmanuel Philibert. Philibert was a prince of superior talents and humane disposition, and the Vaudois cherished the hope that under him they would be permitted to live in peace, and to worship as their fathers had done. What strengthened these just expectations was the fact that Philibert had married a sister of the King of France, Henry II, who had been carefully instructed in the Protestant faith by her illustrious relations, Margaret, Queen of Navarre, and Renee of France, daughter of Louis XII. But, alas! the treaty that restored Emmanuel Philibert to the throne of his ancestors, contained a clause binding the contracting parties to extinguish heresy. This was to send him back to his subjects with a dagger in his hand.

Whatever the king might incline-and, strengthened by the counsels of his Protestant queen, he would doubtless, if he could, have dealt humanely by his faithful subjects, the Vaudois-his intentions were overborne by men of stronger wills and more determined resolves. The inquisitors of his kingdom, the nuncio of the Pope, and the ambassadors of Spain and France, united in urging upon him the purgation of his dominions, in terms of the agreement in the Treaty of Peace. The unhappy monarch, unable to resist these powerful solicitations, issued on the 15th February, 1560, an edict forbidding his subjects to hear the Protestant preachers in the Valley of Lucerna, or anywhere else, under pain of a fine of 100 dollars of gold for the first offence, and of the galleys for life for the second. This edict had reference mainly to the Protestants on the plain of Piedmont, who resorted in crowds to hear sermon in the Valleys. There followed, however, in a short time, a yet severer edict, commanding attendance at mass under pain of death. To carry out this cruel decree, a commission was given to a prince of the blood, Philip of Savoy, Count de Raconis, and with him was associated George Costa, Count de la Trinita, and Thomas Jacomel, the Inquisitor-General, a man as cruel in disposition as he was licentious in manners. To these was added a certain Councillor Corbis, but he was not of the stuff which the business required, and so, after witnessing a few initial scenes of barbarity and horror, he resigned his commission [Monastier, chap. 19, p. 172. Muston, chap. 10, p. 52].

The first burst of the tempest fell on Carignano. This town reposes sweetly on one of the spurs of the Apennines, about twenty miles to the south-west of Turin. It contained many Protestants, some of whom were of good position. The wealthiest were selected and dragged to the burning-pile, in order to strike terror into the rest. The blow had not fallen in vain; the professors of the Protestant creed in Carignano were scattered; some fled to Turin, then under the domination of France, some to other places, and some, alas! frightened by the tempest in front, turned back and sought refuge in the darkness behind them. They had desired the "better country," but could not enter in at the cost of exile and death.

Having done its work in Carignano, this desolating tempest held its way across the plain of Piedmont, towards those great mountains which were the ancient fortress of the truth, marking its track through the villages and country communes in terror, in pillage, and blood. It moved like one of those thunder-clouds which the traveler on the Alps may often descry beneath him, traversing the same plain, and shooting its lightnings earthwards as it advances. Wherever it was known that there was a Vaudois congregation, thither did the cloud turn. And now we behold it at the foot of the Waldensian Alps-at the entrance of the Valleys, within whose mighty natural bulwarks crowds of fugitives from the towns and villages on the plain have already found asylum.

Rumors of the confiscations, arrests, cruel tortures, and horrible deaths which had befallen the Churches at the foot of their mountains, had preceded the appearance of the crusaders at the entrance of the Valleys. The same devastation which had befallen the flourishing Churches on the plain of Piedmont, seemed to impend over the Churches in the bosom of the Alps. At this juncture the pastors and leading laymen assembled to deliberate on the steps to be taken. Having fasted and humbled themselves before God, they sought by earnest prayer the direction of his Holy Spirit [Leger, livr. ii., p. 29.] They resolved to approach the throne of their prince, and by humble remonstrance and petition, set forth the state of their affairs and the justice of their cause. Their first claim was to be heard before being condemned-a right denied to no one accused, however criminal. They next solemnly disclaimed the main offence laid to their charge, that of departing from the true faith, and of adopting doctrines unknown to the Scriptures, and the early ages of the Church. Their faith was that which Christ Himself had taught; which the apostles, following their Great Master, had preached; which the Fathers had vindicated with their pens, and the martyrs with their blood, and which the first four Councils had ratified, and proclaimed to be the faith of the Christian world. From the "old paths," the Bible and all antiquity being witnesses, they had never turned aside; from father to son they had continued these 1,500 years to walk therein.

Their mountains shielded no novelties; they had bowed the knee to no strange gods, and, if they were heretics, so too were the first four Councils; and so too were the apostles themselves. If they erred, it was in the company of the confessors and martyrs of the early ages. They were willing any moment to appeal their cause to a General Council, provided that Council were willing to decide the question by the only infallible standard they knew, the Word of God. If on this evidence they should be convicted of even one heresy, most willingly would they surrender it. On this, the main point of their indictment, what more could they promise? Show us, they said, what the errors are which you ask us to renounce under the penalty of death, and you shall not need to ask a second time.

["First, we do protest before the Almighty and All-just God, before whose tribunal we must all one day appear, that we intend to live and die in the holy faith, piety, and religion of our Lord Jesus Christ, and that we do abhor all heresies that have been, and are, condemned by the Word of God. We do embrace the most holy doctrine of the prophets and apostles, as likewise of the Nicene and Athanasian Creeds; we do subscribe to the four Councils, and to all the ancient Fathers, in all such things as are not repugnant to the analogy of faith." (Leger, livr. ii., pp. 30-1.)]

Their duty to God did not weaken their allegiance to their prince. To piety they added loyalty. The throne before which they now stood had not more faithful and devoted subjects than they. When had they plotted treason, or disputed lawful command of their sovereign? Nay, the more they feared God, the more they honored the king. Their services, their substance, their life, were all at the disposal of their prince; they were willing to lay them all down in defense of his lawful prerogative; one thing only they could not surrender-their conscience.

As regarded their Romanist fellow-subjects of Piedmont, they had lived in good-neighborhood with them. Whose person had they injured-whose property had they robbed-whom had they over-reached in their bargains? Had they not been kind, courteous, honest? If their hills had vied in fertility with the naturally richer plains at their feet, and if their mountain-homes had been filled with store of corn, and oil, and wine, not always found in Piedmontese dwellings, to what was this owing, save to their superior industry, frugality, and skill? Never had marauding expedition descended from their hills to carry off the goods of their neighbors, or to inflict retaliation for the many murders and robberies to which they had had to submit. Why, then, should their neighbors rise against them to exterminate them, as if they were a horde of evil-doers, in whose neighborhood no man could live in peace; and why should their sovereign unsheathe the sword against those who had never been found disturbers of his kingdom, nor plotters against his government, but who, on the contrary, had ever striven to maintain the authority of his law, and the honor of his throne? "One thing is certain, most serene prince," they said, in conclusion, "that the Word of God will not perish, but will abide for ever. If, then, our religion is the pure Word of God, as we are persuaded it is, and not a human invention, no human power will be able to abolish it." [See in Leger (livr. ii., pp. 30-1) the petition of the Vaudois presented "Au Serenissime et tres-Puissant Prince, Philibert Emmanuel, Due de Savoye, Prince de Piemont, notre tres-Clement Seigneur" (To the Serene and most Mighty Prince, Philibert Emmanuel, Duke of Savoy, Prince of Piedmont, our most Gracious Lord).]

Never was there a more solemn, or a more just, or a more respectful remonstrance presented to any throne. The wrong about to be done them was enormous, yet not an angry word, nor a single accusatory sentence, do the Vaudois permit themselves to utter. But to what avail this solemn protest, this triumphant vindication? The more complete and conclusive it is, the more manifest does it make the immense injustice and the flagrant criminality of the House of Savoy. The more the Vaudois put themselves in the right, the more they put the Church of Rome in the wrong; and they who have already doomed them to perish are but the more resolutely determined to carry out their purpose.

This document was accompanied by two others: one to the queen, and one to the Council. The one to the queen is differently conceived from that to the duke. They offer no apology for their faith: the queen herself was of it. They allude in a few touching terms to the sufferings they had already been subjected to, and to the yet greater that appeared to impend. This was enough, they knew, to awaken all her sympathies, and enlist her as their advocate with the king, after the example of Esther, and other noble women in former times, who valued their lofty station less for its dazzling honors, than for the opportunities it gave them of shielding the persecuted confessors of the truth. [See in Leger (livr. ii., p. 32), "A la tres-Vertueuse et tres-Excellente Dame, Madame Marguerite de France, Duchesse de Savoye et de Berry"-"the petition of her poor and humble subjects, the inhabitants of the Valleys of Lucerna and Angrogna, and Perosa and San Martino, and all those of the plain who call purely upon the name of the Lord Jesus."]

The remonstrance presented to the Council was couched in terms more plain and direct, yet still respectful. They bade the counsellors of the king beware what they did; they warned them that every drop of innocent blood they should spill they would one day have to account for; that if the blood of Abel, though only that of one man, cried with a voice so loud that God heard it in heaven, and came down to call its shedder to reckoning, how much mightier the cry that would arise from the blood of a whole nation, and how much more terrible the vengeance with which it would be visited! In fine, they reminded the Council that what they asked was not an unknown privilege in Piedmont, nor would they be the first or the only persons who had enjoyed the indulgence if it should be extended to them. Did not the Jew and the Saracen live unmolested in their cities? Did they not permit the Israelite to build his synagogue, and the Moor to read his Koran, without annoyance or restraint? Was it a great thing that the faith of the Bible should be placed on the same level in this respect with that of the Crescent, and that the descendants of the men who for generations had been the subjects of the House of Savoy, and who had enriched the dominions with their virtues, and defended them with their blood, should be treated with the same humanity that was shown to the alien and the unbeliever?

These petitions the confessors of the Alps dispatched to the proper quarter, and having done so, they waited an answer with eyes lifted up to heaven. If that answer should be peace, with what gratitude to God and to their prince would they hail it! should it be otherwise, they were ready to accept that alternative too; they were prepared to die.

CHAPTER 8
Preparations for a War of Extermination

Where was the Vaudois who would put his life in his hand, and carry this remonstrance to the Duke? The dangerous service was undertaken by M. Gilles, Pastor of Bricherasio, a devoted and courageous man. A companion was associated with him, but wearied out with the rebuffs and insults he met with, he abandoned the mission, and left its conduct to Gilles alone. The duke then lived at Nice, for Turin, his capital, was still in the hands of the French, and the length of the journey very considerably increased its risks. Gilles reached Nice in safety, however, and after many difficulties and delays he had an interview with Queen Margaret, who undertook to place the representations of which he was the bearer in the hands of her husband, the duke. The deputy had an interview also with Philip of Savoy, the duke's brother, and one of the commissioners under the Act for the purgation of the Valleys. The Waldensian pastor was, on the whole, well received by him. Unequally yoked with the cruel and bigoted Count La Trinita, Philip of Savoy soon became disgusted, and left the bloody business wholly in the hands of his fellow-commissioner [Muston, p. 68.] As regarded the queen, her heart was in the Valleys; the cause of the poor Vaudois was her cause also. But she stood alone as their intercessor with the duke; her voice was drowned by the solicitations and threats of the prelates, the King of Spain, and the Pope [Muston, p. 72].

For three months there came neither letter nor edict from the court at Nice. If the men of the Valleys were impatient to know the fate that awaited them, their enemies, athirst for plunder and blood, were still more so. The latter, unable longer to restrain their passions, began persecution on their own account. They thought they knew their sovereign's intentions, and made bold to anticipate them.

The tocsin was rung out from the Monastery of Pinerolo. Perched on the frontier of the Valleys, the monks of this establishment kept their eyes fixed upon the heretics of the mountains, as vultures watch their prey, ever ready to sweep down upon hamlet or valley when they found it unguarded. They hired a troop of marauders, whom they sent forth to pillage. The band returned, driving before them a wretched company of captives, whom they had dragged from their homes and vineyards in the mountains. The poorer sort they burnt alive, or sent to the galleys; the rich they imprisoned till they had paid the ransom to which they were held [Muston, p. 69. Monastier, p. 178].

The example of the monks was followed by certain Popish landlords in the Valley of San Martino. The two seigneurs of Perrier attacked, before day-break of April 2nd, 1560, the villagers of Rioclareto, with an armed band. Some they slaughtered, the rest they drove out, without clothes or food, to perish on the snow-clad hills. The ruffians who had expelled them took possession of their dwellings, protesting that no one should enter them unless he were willing to go to mass. They kept possession only three days, for the Protestants of the Valley of Clusone, to the number of 400, hearing of the outrage, crossed the mountains, drove out the invaders, and reinstated their brethren [Muston, p. 70. Monastier, pp. 176-7].

Next appeared in the Valleys, Philip of Savoy, Count de Raconis, and Chief Commissioner. He was an earnest Roman Catholic, but a humane and upright man. He attended sermon one day in the Protestant church of Angrogna, and was so much pleased with what he heard, that he obtained from the pastor an outline of the Vaudois faith, so as to send it to Rome, in the hope that the Pope would cease to persecute a creed that seemed so little heretical. A sanguine hope truly! Where the honest count had seen very little heresy, the Pope, Pius IV., saw a great deal; and would not even permit a disputation with the Waldensian pastors, as the count had proposed. He would stretch his benignity no further than to absolve "from their past crimes" all who were willing to enter the Church of Rome.   This was not very encouraging, still the count did not abandon his idea of conciliation. In June,

1560, he came a second time to the Valley of Lucerna, accompanied by his colleague, La Trinita, and assembling the pastors and heads of families, he told them that the persecution would cease immediately, provided they would consent to hear the preachers he had brought with him, Brothers of the Christian Doctrine. He further proposed that they should silence their own ministers while they were making trial of his. The Vaudois expressed their willingness to consent, provided the count's ministers preached the pure Gospel; but if they preached human traditions, they (the Vaudois) would be under the necessity of withholding their consent; and, as regarded silencing their own ministers, it was only reasonable that they should be permitted first to make trial of the count's preachers. A few days after, they had a taste of the new expositors. Selecting the ablest among them, they made him ascend the pulpit, and hold forth to a Vaudois congregation. He took a very effectual way to make them listen. "I will demonstrate to you," said he, "that the mass is found in Scripture. The word massah signifies 'sent,' does it not?" "Not precisely," replied his hearers, who knew more about Hebrew than was convenient for the preacher. "The primitive expression," continued he, "Ite missa est, was employed to dismiss the auditory, was it not?" "That is quite true," replied his hearers, without very clearly seeing how it bore on his argument. "Well, then, you see, gentlemen, that the mass is found in the Holy Scripture" [Muston, p. 71. Monastier, pp. 177-8]. The congregation were unable to determine whether the preacher was arguing with them, or simply laughing at them.

Finding the Waldenses obdurate, as he deemed them, the Duke of Savoy, in October, 1560, declared war against them. Early in that month a dreadful rumor reached the Valleys, namely, that the duke was levying an army to exterminate them. The news was but too true. The duke offered a free pardon to all "outlaws, convicts, and vagabonds" who would enroll as volunteers to serve against the Vaudois. Soon an army of a truly dreadful character was assembled. The Vaudois seemed doomed to total and inevitable destruction. The pastors and chief persons assembled to deliberate on the measures to be taken at this terrible crisis. Feeling that their refuge was in God alone, they resolved that they would take no means for deliverance which might be offensive to him, or dishonorable to themselves. The pastors were to exhort every one to apply to God, with true faith, sincere repentance, and ardent prayer; and as to defensive measures, they recommended that each family should collect their provisions, clothes, utensils, and herds, and be ready at a moment's notice to convey them, together with all infirm persons, to their strongholds in the mountains. Meanwhile, the duke's army-if the collected ruffianism of Piedmont could be so called-came nearer every day [Muston, p. 72. Monastier, p. 182].

On the 31st of October, a proclamation was posted throughout the Valley of Angrogna, calling on the inhabitants to return within the Roman pale, under penalty of extermination by fire and sword. On the day following, the 1st of November, the Papal army appeared at Bubiana, on the right bank of the Pelice, at the entrance to the Waldensian Valleys. The host numbered 4,000 infantry and 200 horses; comprising, besides the desperadoes that formed its main body, a few veterans, who had seen a great deal of service in the wars with France [Letter of Scipio Lentullus, Pastor of San Giovanni. (Leger, Hist. des Eglises Vaud., livr. ii., p. 35.)]

The Vaudois, the enemy being now in sight, humbled themselves, in a public fast, before God. Next, they partook together of the Lord's Supper. Refreshed in soul by these services, they proceeded to put in execution the measures previously resolved on. The old men and the women climbed the mountains, awakening the echoes with the psalms which they sung on their way to the Pra del Tor, within whose natural ramparts of rock and snow-clad peaks they sought asylum. The Vaudois population of the Valleys at that time was not more than 18,000; their armed men did not exceed 1,200; these were distributed at various passes and barricades to oppose the enemy, who was now near. [So says the Pastor of Giovanni, Scipio Lentullus, in the letter already referred to. (Leger, livr. ii., p. 35.)]

On the 2nd of November the Piedmontese army, putting itself in motion, crossed the Pelice, and advanced along the narrow defile that leads up to the Valleys, having the heights of Bricherasio on the right, and the spurs of Monte Friolante on the left, with the towering masses of the Vandalin and Castelluzzo in front. The Piedmontese encamped in the meadows of San Giovanni, within a stone's-throw of the point where the Val di Lucerna and the Val di Angrogna divide, the former to expand into a noble breadth of meadow and vineyard, running on between magnificent mountains, with their rich clothing of pastures, chestnut groves, and chalets, till it ends in the savage Pass of Miraboue; and the latter to wind and climb in a grand succession of precipice, and gorge, and grassy dell, till it issues in the funnel-shaped valley around which the ice-crowned mountains stand the everlasting sentinels.

It was the latter of these two valleys (Angrogna) that La Trinita first essayed to enter. He marched 1,200 men into it, the wings of his army deploying over its bordering heights of La Cotiere. His soldiers were opposed by only a small body of Vaudois, some of whom were armed solely with the sling and the cross-bow. Skirmishing with the foe, the Vaudois retired, fighting, to the higher grounds. When the evening set in, neither side could claim a decided advantage. Wearied with skirmishing, both armies encamped for the night-the Vaudois on the heights of Roccomaneot, and the Piedmontese, their camp-fires lighted, on the lower hills of La Cotiere.

Suddenly the silence of the evening was startled by a derisive shout that rose from the Piedmontese host. What had happened to evoke these sounds of contempt? They had descried, between them and the sky, on the heights above them, the bending figures of the Vaudois. On their knees, the Waldensian warriors were supplicating the God of battles. Hardly had the scoffs with which the Piedmontese hailed the act died away, when a drum was heard to beat in a side valley. A child had got hold of the instrument, and was amusing itself with it. The soldiers of La Trinita saw in imagination a fresh body of Waldensians advancing from this lateral defile to rush upon them. They seized their arms in no little disorder. The Vaudois, seeing the movement of the foe, seized theirs also, and rushed down-hill to anticipate the attack. The Piedmontese threw away their arms and fled, chased by the Waldenses, thus losing in half an hour the ground it had cost them a day's fighting to gain. The weapons abandoned by the fugitives formed a much-needed and most opportune supply to the Vaudois. As the result of the combats of the day, La Trinita had sixty-seven men slain; of the Vaudois, three only had fallen [Letter of Scipio Lentullus. (Leger, livr. ii., p. 25.) Muston, pp. 73-4].

Opening on the left of La Trinita was the corn-clad, vine-clad, and mountain-ramparted Valley of Lucerna, with its towns, La Torre, Villaro, Bobbio, and others, forming the noblest of the Waldensian Valleys. La Trinita now occupied this valley with his soldiers. This was comparatively an easy achievement, almost all its inhabitants having fled to the Pra del Tor. Those that remained were mostly Romanists, who were, at that time, mixed with the Waldensian population, and even they, committing their wives and daughters to the keeping of their Vaudois neighbors, had sent them with them to the Pra del Tor, to escape the brutal outrages of the Papal army. On the following days La Trinita fought some small affairs with the Vaudois, in all of which he was repulsed with considerable slaughter. The arduous nature of the task he had in hand now began to dawn upon him.

The mountaineers, he saw, were courageous, and determined to die rather than submit their conscience to the Pope, and their families to the passions of his soldiers. He discovered, moreover, that they were a simple and confiding people, utterly unversed in the ways of intrigue. He was delighted to find these qualities in them, because he thought he saw how he could turn them to account. He had tools with him as cunning and vile as himself-Jacomel, the inquisitor; and Gastand, his secretary; the latter feigned a love for the Gospel. These men he set to work. When they had prepared matters, he assembled the leading men of the Waldenses, and recited to them some flattering words, which he had heard, or professed to have heard, the duke and duchess make use of towards them; he protested that this was no pleasant business in which he was engaged, and that he would be glad to have it off his hands; peace, he thought, could easily be arranged, if they would only make a few small concessions to show that they were reasonable men; he would propose that they should deposit their arms in the house of one of their syndics, and permit him, for form's sake, to go with a small train, and celebrate mass in the Church of St. Laurenzo, in Angrogna, and afterwards pay a visit to the Pra del Tor. La Trinita's proposal proved the correctness of the estimate he had formed of Vaudois confidingness. The people spent a whole night in deliberating over the count's proposition, and, contrary to the opinion of their pastors and some of their laymen, agreed to accept it [Leger, livr. ii., p. 35. Monastier, pp. 184-5].

The Papal general said his mass in the Protestant church. After this he traversed the gloomy defiles that led up to the famous Pra, on whose green slopes, with their snowy battlements, he was so desirous to feast his eyes; though, it is said, he showed evident trepidation when he passed the black pool of Tompie, with its memories of retribution. Having accomplished these feats in safety, he returned to wear the mask a little longer.

He resumed the efforts on which he professed to be so earnestly and laudably bent, of effecting peace. The duke had now come nearer, and was living at Vercelli, on the plain of Piedmont; La Trinita thought that the Vaudois ought by all means to send deputies thither. It would strengthen their supplication-indeed, all but insure its success-if they would raise a sum of 20,000 crowns. On payment of this sum he would withdraw his army, and leave them to practice their religion in peace [Leger, livr. ii., p. 35]. The Vaudois, unable to conceive of dissimulation like La Trinita's, made concession after concession. They had previously laid down their arms; they now sent deputies to the duke; next they taxed themselves to buy off his soldiers; and last, and worst of all, at the demand of La Trinita, they sent away their pastors. It was dreadful to think of a journey across the Col Julien at that season; yet it had to be gone. Over its snowy summits, where the winter drifts were continually obliterating the track, and piling up fresh wreaths; across the Valleys of Prali and San Martino, and over the ice-clad mountains beyond, had this sorrowful band of pastors to pursue their way, to find refuge among the Protestants in the French Valley of Pragelas. This difficult and dangerous route was forced upon them, the more direct road through the Valley of Perosa being closed by the marauders and assassins that infested it, and especially by those in the pay of the monks of Pinerolo.

The count believed that the poor people were now entirely in his power. His soldiers did their pleasure in the Valley of Lucerna. They pillaged the houses abandoned by the Vaudois. The few inhabitants who had remained, as well as those who had returned, thinking that during the negotiations for peace hostilities would be suspended, were fain to make their escape a second time, and to seek refuge in the woods and caves of the higher reaches of the Valleys. The outrages committed by the ruffians to whom the Valley of Lucerna was now given over were of a kind that cannot be told. The helpless man, who had lived a hundred and three years, was placed in a cave, and his granddaughter, a girl of seventeen, was left to take care of him. The soldiers found out his hiding-place; the old man was murdered, and outrage was offered to his granddaughter. She fled from the brutal pursuit of the soldiers, leaped over a precipice and died. In another instance, an old man was pursued to a brink of a precipice by one of La Trinita's soldiers. The Vaudois had no alternative but to throw himself over the brink or die by the sword of his pursuer. He stopped, turned round, and dropped on his knees, as if to supplicate for his life. The trooper was raising his sword to strike him dead, when the Vaudois clasping him tightly round the legs, and swaying himself backwards with all his might, rolled over the precipice, dragging the soldier with him into the abyss.

Part of the sum agreed upon between La Trinita and the Waldenses had now been paid to him. To raise this money the poor people were under the necessity of selling their herds. The count now withdrew his army into winter quarters at Cavour, a point so near the Valleys that a few hours' march would enable him to re-enter them at any moment. The corn, and oil, and wine he had not been able to carry away he destroyed. Even the mills he broke in pieces. His design appeared to be to leave the Vaudois only the alternative of submission, or of dying of hunger on their mountains. To afflict them yet more, he placed garrisons here and there in the Valleys; and, in the very wantonness of tyranny, required those who were themselves without bread to provide food for his soldiers. These soldiers were continually prowling about in search of victims on whom to gratify their cruelty and their lust. Those who had the unspeakable misfortune to be dragged into their den, had to undergo, if men, excruciating torture; if women, revolting outrage [Muston, p. 77. Monastier, pp. 186-7].

CHAPTER 9
The Great Campaign of 1561

These frightful inflictions the Waldenses had submitted to, in the hope that the deputies whom they had sent to the duke would bring back with them an honorable peace. The impatience with which they waited their return may well be conceived. At last, after an absence of six weeks, the commissioners reappeared in the Valleys; but their dejected faces, even before they had uttered a word, told that they had not succeeded. They had been sent back with an order, enjoining on the Vaudois unconditional submission to the church of Rome on pain of extermination. To enforce that order to the uttermost a more numerous army was at that moment being raised. The mass or universal slaughter-such was the alternative now presented to them.

The spirit of the people woke up. Rather than thus disgrace their ancestors, imperil their own souls, and entail a heritage of slavery on their children, they would die a thousand times. Their depression was gone; they were as men who had awakened from heavy sleep; they had found their arms. Their first care was to recall their pastors, their next to raise up their fallen churches, and their third to resume public service in them. Daily their courage grew, and once more joy lighted up their faces.

There came letters of sympathy and promises of help from their fellow-Protestants of Geneva, Dauphine, and France. Over the two latter countries persecution at that hour impended, but their own dangers made them all the more ready to succor their brethren of the Valleys. "Thereupon," says an historian, "took place one of those grand and solemn scenes, which, at once heroic and religious, seem rather adapted for an epic poem than for grave history" [Muston, p. 78].

The Waldenses of Lucerna sent deputies across the mountains, then covered to a great depth with snow, to propose an alliance with the Protestants of the Valley of Pragelas, who were at that time threatened by their sovereign, Francis I. The proposed alliance was joyfully accepted. Assembling on a plateau of snow facing the mountains of Descriers, and the chain of the Guinevere, the deputies swore to stand by each other, and render mutual support in the coming struggle [Monastier, p. 188. Muston, p. 78]. It was agreed that this oath of alliance should be sworn with a like solemnity in the Waldensian Valleys.

The deputies from Pragelas, crossing the Mount Julien, arrived at Bobbio on the 21st January, 1561. Their coming was singularly opportune. On the evening before, a ducal proclamation had been published in the Valleys, commanding the Vaudois, within twenty-four hours, to give attendance at mass, or abide the consequences-"fire, sword, the cord: the three arguments of Romanism," says Muston. This was the first news with which the Prerelease deputies were met on their arrival. With all the more enthusiasm they proceeded to renew their oath. Ascending a low hill behind Bobbio, the deputies from Pragelas, and those from Lucerna, standing erect in the midst of the assembled heads of families, who knelt around, pronounced these words-

> "In the name of the Vaudois Churches of the Alps, of Dauphine, and of Piedmont, which have ever been united, and of which we are the representatives, we here promise, our hands on our Bibles, and in the presence of God, that all our Valleys shall courageously sustain each other in matters of religion, without prejudice to the obedience due to their legitimate superiors.
>
> "We promise to maintain the Bible, whole and without admixture, according to the usage of the true Apostolic Church, persevering in this holy religion, though it be at the peril of our life, in order that we may transmit it to our children, intact and pure, as we received it from our fathers.
>
> "We promise aid and succor to our persecuted brothers, not regarding our individual interests, but the common cause; and not relying upon man, but upon God" [Muston, pp. 78-9].

The physical grandeurs of the spot were in meet accordance with the moral sublimity of the transaction. Immediately beneath was spread out the green bosom of the valley, with here and there the silver of the Pelice gleaming out amid vineyards and acacia-groves. Filling the horizon on all sides save one stood up an array of magnificent mountains, white with the snows of winter. Conspicuous among them were the grand peaks of the Col de Mauler and the Col de la Croix. They looked the silent and majestic witnesses of the oath in which a heroic people bound themselves to die rather than permit the defilement of their hearths, and the profanation of their altars, by the hordes of an idolatrous tyranny. It was in this grand fashion that the Waldenses opened one of the most brilliant campaigns ever waged by their arms.

The next morning, according to the duke's order, they must choose between the mass and the penalty annexed to refusal. A neighboring church-one of those which had been taken from them-stood ready, with altar decked and tapers lighted, for the Vaudois to hear their first mass. Hardly had the day dawned when the expected penitents were at the church door. They would show the duke in what fashion they meant to read their recantation. They entered the building. A moment they stood surveying the strange transformation their church had undergone, and then they set to work. To extinguish the tapers, pull down the images, and sweep into the street rosary, and crucifix, and all the other paraphernalia of the Popish worship, was but the work of a few minutes. The minister, Hubert Arts, then ascended the pulpit, and reading out as his text Isaiah xlv. 20--"Assemble yourselves and come; draw near together, ye that are escaped of the nations: they have no knowledge that set up the wood of their graven image, and pray unto a God that cannot save"-preached a sermon which struck the key-note of the campaign then opening.

The inhabitants of the hamlets and chalets in the mountains rushed down, like their own winter torrents, into Lucerna, and the army of the Vaudois reinforced, set out to purge the temple at Villaro. On their way they encountered the Piedmontese garrison. They attacked and drove them back; the monks, seigneurs, and magistrates, who had come to receive the abjuration of the heretics, accompanying the troops in their ignominious flight. The whole band of fugitives-soldiers, priests, and judges-shut themselves up in the town of Villaro, which was now besieged by the Vaudois. Thrice did the garrison from La Torre attempt to raise the siege, and thrice were they repulsed. At last, on the tenth day, the garrison surrendered, and had their lives spared, two Waldensian pastors accompanying them to La Torre, the soldiers expressing greater confidence in them than in any other escort.

The Count La Trinita, seeing his garrison driven out, struck his encampment at Cavour, and moved his army into the Valleys. He again essayed to sow dissension amongst the Vaudois by entangling them in negotiations for peace, but by this time they had learned too well the value of his promises to pay the least attention to them, or to intermit for an hour their preparations for defense. It was now the beginning of February, 1561.

The Vaudois labored with the zeal of men who feel that their cause is a great and a righteous one, and are prepared to sacrifice all for it. They erected barricades; they planted ambushes; they appointed signals, to telegraph the movements of the enemy from post to post. "Every house," says Muston, "became a manufactory of pikes, bullets, and other weapons." They selected the best marksmen their Valleys could furnish, and formed them into the "Flying Company," whose duty it was to hasten to the point where the danger pressed the most. To each body of fighting men they attached two pastors, to maintain the morale of their army. The pastors, morning and evening, led the public devotions; they prayed with the soldiers before going into battle; and when the fighting was over, and the Vaudois were chasing the enemy down their great mountains, and through their dark gorges, they exerted themselves to prevent the victory from being stained by any unnecessary effusion of blood.

La Trinita knew well that if he would subjugate the Valleys, and bring the campaign to a successful end, he must make himself master of the Pra del Tor. Into that vast natural citadel was now gathered the main body of the Waldensian people. What of their herds and provisions remained to them had been transported thither; there they had constructed mills and baking-ovens; there, too, sat their council, and thence directed the whole operations of the defense. A blow struck there would crush the Vaudois' heart, and convert what the Waldenses regarded as their impregnable castle into their tomb.

Deferring the chastisement of the other valleys meanwhile, La Trinita directed all his efforts against Angrogna. His first attempt to enter it with his army was made on the 4th February. The fighting lasted till night, and ended in his repulse. His second attempt, three days after, carried him some considerable way into Angrogna, burning and ravaging, but his partial success cost him dear, and the ground won had ultimately to be abandoned [Monastier, p. 190. Muston, p. 80].

The 14th of February saw the severest struggle. Employing all his strategy to make himself master of the much-coveted Pra, with all in it, he divided his army into three corps, and advanced against it from three points. One body of troops, marching along the gorges of the Angrogna, and traversing the narrow chasm that leads up to the Pra, attacked it on the south. Another body, climbing the heights from Pramol, and crossing the snowy flanks of La Vechera, tried to force an entrance on the east; while a third, ascending from San Martino, and crossing the lofty summits that wall in the Pra on the north, descended upon it from that quarter. The count's confident expectation was that if his men should be unable to force an entrance at one point, they were sure to do so at another.

No scout had given warning of what was approaching. While three armies were marching to attack them, the Waldenses, in their grand valley, with its rampart of ice-crowned peaks, were engaged in their morning devotions. Suddenly the cries of fugitives, and the shouts of assailants, issuing from the narrow chasm on the south, broke upon their ear, together with the smoke of burning hamlets. Of the three points of attack, this was the easiest to be defended. Six brave Waldensian youths strode down the valley, to stop the way against La Trinita's soldiers. They were six against an army.

The road by which the soldiers were advancing is long and gloomy, and overhung by great rocks, and so narrow that only two men can march abreast. On this side rises the mountain; on that, far down, thunders the torrent; a ledge in the steep face of the cliff, running here in the darkness, there in the sunshine, serves as a pathway. It leads to what is termed the gate of the Pra. That gateway is formed by an angle of the mountain, which obtrudes upon the narrow ledge on the one side, while a huge rock rises on the other, and still further narrows the point of ingress into the Pra del Tor. Access into the famous Pra, of which La Trinita was now striving to make himself master, there is not on this side, save through this narrow opening; seeing that on the right rises the mountain; on the left yawns the gulf, into which, if one steps aside but in the least, he tumbles headlong. to friend and foe alike the only entrance into the Pra del Tor on the south is by this gate of Nature's own erecting. It was here that the six Waldensian warriors took their stand [Monastier, p. 191]. Immovable as their own Alps, they not only checked the advance of the host, but drove it back in a panic-stricken mass, which made the precipices of the defile doubly fatal.

Others would have hastened to their aid, had not danger suddenly presented itself in another quarter. On the heights of La Vechera, crossing the snow, was descried an armed troop, making their entrance into the valley on the east. Before they had time to descend they were met by the Waldenses, who dispersed them and made them flee. Two of the attacking parties of the count have failed; will the third have better success?

As the Waldenses were pursuing the routed enemy on La Vechera, they saw yet another armed troop, which had crossed the mountains that separate the Val San Martino from the Pra del Tor on the north, descending upon them. Instantly the alarm was raised. A few men only could they dispatch to meet the invaders. These lay in ambush at the mouth of a defile through which the attacking party was making its way down into the Pra. Emerging from the defile, and looking down into the valley beneath them, they exclaimed, "Haste, haste! Angrogna is ours." The Vaudois, starting up and crying out, "It is you that are ours," rushed upon them sword in hand. Trusting to their superior numbers, the Piedmontese soldiers fought desperately. But a few minutes sufficed for the men of the Valleys to hurry from the points where they were now victorious, to the assistance of their brethren. The invaders, seeing themselves attacked on all sides, turned and fled up the slopes they had just descended. Many were slain, nor would a man of them have re-crossed the mountains but for the pastor of the Flying Company, who, raising his voice to the utmost pitch, entreated the pursuers to spare the lives of those who were no longer able to resist. Among the slain was Charles Truchet, who so cruelly ravaged the commune of Rioclaret a few months before. A stone from a sling laid him prostrate on the ground, and his head was cut off with his own sword. Louis de Monteuil, another noted persecutor of the Vaudois, perished in the same action.

Furious at his repulse, the count La Trinita turned his arms against the almost defenseless Valley of Rora. He ravaged it, burning its little town, and chasing away its population of eighty families, who escaped over the snows of the mountains to Villaro, in the Valley of Lucerna. That valley he next entered with his soldiers, and though it was for the moment almost depopulated, the Popish general received so warm a welcome from those peasants who remained that, after being again and again beaten, he was fain to draw off his men-at-arms, and retreat to his old quarters at Cavour, there to chew the cud over his misfortunes, and hatch new stratagems and plan new attacks, which he fondly hoped would retrieve his disgraces.

La Trinita spent a month in reinforcing his army, greatly weakened by the losses it had sustained. The King of France sent him ten companies of foot, and some other choice soldiers [Leger, part ii., p. 36. Gilles, chap. 25.] There came a regiment from Spain; and numerous volunteers from Piedmont, comprising many of the nobility. From 4,000, the original number of his army, it was now raised to 7,000 [Ibid., part ii., p. 37]. He thought himself strong enough to begin a third campaign. He was confident that this time he would wipe out the disgrace which had befallen his arms, and sweep from the earth at once and for ever the great scandal of the Waldenses. He again directed all his efforts against Angrogna, the heart and bulwark of the Valleys.

It was Sunday, the 17th of March, 1561. The whole of the Vaudois assembled in the Pra del Tor had met on the morning of that day, soon after dawn, as was their wont, to unite in public devotion. The first rays of the rising sun were beginning to light up the white hills around them, and the last cadences of their morning psalm were dying away on the grassy slopes of the Pra, when a sudden alarm was raised. The enemy was approaching by three routes. On the ridges of the eastern summits appeared one body of armed men; another was defiling up the chasm, and in a few minutes would pour itself, through the gateway already described, into the Pra; while a third was forcing itself over the rocks by a path intermediate between the two. Instantly the enemy was met on all the points of approach. A handful of Waldensians sufficed to thrust back along the narrow gorge the line of glittering cuirassed men, who were defiling through it. At the other two points, where bastions of rock and earth had been erected, the fighting was severe, and the dead lay thick, but the day at both places went against the invaders. Some of the ablest captains were among the slain. The number of the soldiers killed was so great that Count La Trinita is said to have sat down and wept when he beheld the heaps of the dead [Muston, p. 83]. It was matter of astonishment at the time that the Waldenses did not pursue the invaders, for had they done so, being so much better acquainted with the mountain-paths, not one of all that host would have been left alive to carry tidings of its discomfiture to the inhabitants of Piedmont. Their pastors restrained the victorious Vaudois, having laid it down as a maxim at the beginning of the campaign that they would use with moderation and clemency whatever victories the "God of battles" might be pleased to give them, and that they would spill no blood unless when absolutely necessary to prevent their own being shed. The number of slain Piedmontese was again out of all proportion to those who had fallen on the other side; so much so, that it was currently said in the cities of Piedmont that "God was fighting for the barbets" [Ibid. Monastier, p. 194].

More deeply humiliated and disgraced than ever, La Trinita led back the remains of his army to its old quarters. Well had it been for him if he had never set foot within the Waldensian territory, and not less so for many of those who followed him, including not a few of the nobles of Piedmont, whose bones were now bleaching on the mountains of the Vaudois. But the Popish general was slow to learn the lesson of these events. Even yet he harbored the design of returning to assail that fatal valley where he had lost so many laurels, and buried so many soldiers; but he covered his purpose with craft. Negotiations had been opened between the men of the Valleys and the Duke of Savoy, and as they were proceeding satisfactorily, the Vaudois were without suspicions of evil. This was the moment that La Trinita chose to attack them. He hastily assembled his troops, and on the night of the 16th April he marched them against the Pra del Tor, hoping to enter it unopposed, and give the Vaudois "as sheep to the slaughter."

The snows around the Pra were beginning to burn in the light of morning when the attention of the people, who had just ended their united worship, was attracted by unusual sounds which were heard to issue from the gorge that led into the valley. On the instant six brave mountaineers rushed to the gateway that opens from the gorge. The long file of La Trinita's soldiers was seen advancing two abreast, their helmets and cuirasses glittering in the light. The six Vaudois made their arrangements, and calmly waited till the enemy was near. The first two Vaudois, holding loaded muskets, knelt down. The second two stood erect, ready to fire over the heads of the first two. The third two undertook the loading of the weapons as they were discharged. The invaders came on. As the first two of the enemy turned the rock they were shot down by the two foremost Vaudois. The next two of the attacking force fell in like manner by the shot of the Vaudois in the rear. The third rank of the enemy presented themselves only to be laid by the side of their comrades. In a few minutes a little heap of dead bodies blocked the pass, rendering impossible the advance of the accumulating file of the enemy in the chasm.

Meanwhile, other Vaudois climbed the mountains that overhang the gorge in which the Piedmontese arm was imprisoned. Tearing up the great stones with which the hill-side was strewn, the Vaudois sent them rolling down upon the host. Unable to advance from the wall of dead in front, and unable to flee from the ever-accumulating masses behind, the soldiers were crushed in dozens by the falling rocks. Panic set in: and panic in such a position was dreadful. Wedged together on the narrow ledge, with a murderous rain of rocks falling on them, their struggle to escape was frightful. They jostled one another, and trod each other under foot, while vast numbers fell over the precipice, and were dashed on the rocks or drowned in the torrent [Leger, part ii., p. 37. Muston, p. 85]. When those at the entrance of the valley, who were watching the result, saw the crystal of the Angrogna begin about midday to be changed into blood, "Ah!" said they, "the Pra del Tor has been taken; La Trinita has triumphed; there flows the blood of the Vaudois." And, indeed, the count on beginning his march that morning is said to have boasted that by noon the torrent of the Angrogna would be seen to change color; and so in truth it did. Instead of a pellucid stream, rolling along on a white gravelly bed, which is its usual appearance at the mouth of the valley, it was now deeply dyed from recent slaughter. But when the few who had escaped the catastrophe returned to tell what had that day passed within the defiles of the Angrogna, it was seen that it was not the blood of the Vaudois, but the blood of their ruthless invaders, which dyed the waters of the Angrogna. The count withdrew on that same night with his army, to return no more to the Valleys.

Negotiations were again resumed, not this time through the Count La Trinita, but through Philip of Savoy, Count of Raconis, and were speedily brought to a satisfactory issue. The Duke of Savoy had but small merit in making peace with the men whom he found he could not conquer. The capitulation was signed on the 5th of June, 1561, and its first clause granted an indemnity for all offences. It is open to remark that this indemnity was given to those who had suffered, not to those who had committed the offences it condoned. The articles that followed permitted the Vaudois to erect churches in their Valleys, with the exception of two or three of their towns, and to hold public worship-in short, to celebrate all the offices of their religion. All the "ancient franchises, immunities, and privileges, whether conceded by his Highness, or by his Highness's predecessors," were renewed, provided they were vouched by public documents [the Articles of Capitulation are given in full in Leger, part ii., pp. 38-40]. Such was the arrangement that closed this war of fifteen months. The Vaudois ascribed it in great part to the influence of the good Duchess Margaret. The Pope designated it a "pernicious example," which he feared would not want imitators in those times when the love of many to the Roman See was waxing cold. It stank in the nostrils of the prelates and monks of Piedmont, to whom the heretics had been a free booty. Nevertheless, Duke Emanuel Philibert faithfully maintained its stipulations, the duchess being by his side to counteract any pressure in the contrary direction. This peace, together with the summer that was now opening, began to slowly efface the deep scars persecution had left on the Valleys; and what further helped to console and reanimate this brave but afflicted people, were the sympathy and aid universally tendered them by Protestants abroad, in particular by Calvin and the Elector Palatine, the latter addressing a spirited letter to the duke on behalf of his persecuted subjects [Leger, part ii., p. 41].

Nothing was more admirable than the spirit of devotion which the Vaudois exhibited all through these terrible conflicts. Their Valleys resounded not less with the voice of prayer and praise, than with the din of arms. Their opponents came from carousing, from blaspheming, from murdering, to engage in battle; the Waldenses rose from their knees to unsheathe the sword, and wield it in a cause which they firmly believed to be that of Him to whom they had bent in supplication. When their little army went a-field their barbes always accompanied it, to inspirit the soldiers by suitable exhortations before joining battle, and to moderate in the hour of victory a vengeance which, however excusable, would yet have tarnished the glory of the triumph. When the fighting men hastened to the bastion or to the defile, the pastors betook themselves to the mountain's slope, or to its summit, and there with uplifted hands supplicated help from the "Lord, strong and mighty, the Lord mighty in battle." When the battle had ceased, and the enemy were in flight, and the victors had returned from chasing their invaders from their Valleys, the grey-haired pastor, the lion-hearted man of battle, the matron, the maiden, the stripling, and the little child, would assemble in Pra del Tor, and while the setting sun was kindling into glory the mountain-tops of their once more ransomed land, they would raise their voices together, and sing the old war-song of Judah, in strains so heroic that the great rocks around them would send back the thunder of their praise in louder echoes than those of the battle whose triumphant issue they were celebrating.

CHAPTER 10
Waldensian Colonies in Calabria and Apulia

One day, about the year 1340, two Waldensian youths were seated in an inn in Turin, engaged in earnest conversation respecting their home prospects. Shut up in their valleys, and cultivating with toil their somewhat sterile mountains, they sighed for wider limits and a more fertile land. "Come with me," said a stranger, who had been listening unperceived to their discourse, "Come with me, and I will give you fertile fields for your barren rocks." The person who now courteously addressed the youths, and whose steps Providence had directed to the same hotel with themselves, was a gentleman from Calabria, at the southern extremity of the Italian Peninsula.

On their return to the Valleys the youths reported the words of the stranger, and the flattering hopes he had held out should they be willing to migrate to this southern land, where skies more genial, and an earth more fertile, would reward their labor with more bounteous harvests. The elders of the Vaudois people listened not without interest. The population of their Valleys had recently been largely increased by numbers of Albigensian refugees, who had escaped from the massacres of Innocent III in the south of France; and the Waldenses, feeling themselves overcrowded, were prepared to welcome any fair scheme that promised an enlargement of their boundaries. But before acceding to the proposition of the stranger, they thought it advisable to send competent persons to examine this new and to them unknown land. The Vaudois explorers returned with a flattering account of the conditions and capabilities of the country they had been invited to occupy. Compared with their own more northern mountains, whose summits

93

Winter covered all the year through with his snows, whose gorges were swept by furious gusts, and whose sides were stripped of their corn and vines by devastating torrents, Calabria was a land of promise. "There are beautiful hills," says the historian Gilles, describing this settlement, "clothed with all kinds of fruit-trees spontaneously springing up according to their situation–in the plains, vines and chestnuts; on the rising ground, walnuts and every fruit-tree. Everywhere were seen rich arable land and few laborers." A considerable body of emigrants set out for this new country. The young men were accompanied to their future homes with partners. They carried with them the Bible in the Romance version, "that holy ark of the New Covenant, and of everlasting peace."

The conditions of their emigration offered a reasonable security for the free and undisturbed exercise of their worship. "By a convention with the local seigneurs, ratified later by the King of Naples, Ferdinand of Arragon, they were permitted to govern their own affairs, civil and spiritual, by their own magistrates, and their own pastors" [Muston, p. 37]. Their first settlement was near the town of Montalto. Half a century later rose the city of San Sexto, which afterwards became the capital of the colony. Other towns and villages sprang up, the region, which before had been thinly inhabited, and but poorly cultivated, was soon transformed into a smiling garden. The swelling hills were clothed with fruit-trees, and the plains waved with luxuriant crops. The Marquis of Spinello was so struck with the prosperity and wealth of the settlements that he offered to cede lands on his own vast and fertile estates where these colonists might build cities and plant vineyards. One of their towns he authorized them to surround with a wall; hence its name, La Guardia. This town, situated on a height near the sea, soon became populous and opulent [Leger, part ii., p. 333].

Towards the close of the same century, another body of Vaudois emigrants from Provence arrived in the south of Italy. The new-comers settled in Apulia, not far from their Calabrian brethren. Villages and towns arose, and the region speedily put on a new face under the improved arts and husbandry of the colonists. Their smiling homes, which looked forth from amid groves of orange and myrtle, their hills covered with the olive and the vine, their corn-fields and pasture-lands, were the marvel and the envy of their neighbors.

In 1500 there arrived in Calabria yet another emigration from the Valleys of Pragelas and Fraissinieres. This third body of colonists established themselves on the Volturata, a river which flows from the Apennines into the Bay of Tarento. With the increase of their numbers came an increase of prosperity to the colonists. Their neighbors, who knew not the secret of this prosperity, were lost in wonder and admiration of it. The physical attributes of the region occupied by the emigrants differed in no respect from those of their own lands, both were placed under the same sky, but how different the aspect of the one from that of the other! The soil, touched by the plough of the Vaudois, seemed to feel a charm that made it open its bosom and yield a tenfold increase. The vine tended by Vaudois hands bore richer clusters, and strove in generous rivalry with the fig and the olive to outdo them in enriching with its produce the Vaudois board. And how delightful the quiet and order of their towns; and the air of happiness on the faces of the people! And how sweet to listen to the bleating of the flocks on the hills, the lowing of the herds in the meadows, the song of the reaper and grape-gatherer, and the merry voices of children at play around the hamlets and villages! For about 200 years these colonies continued to flourish.

"It is a curious circumstance," says the historian M'Crie, "that the first gleam of light, at the revival of letters, shone on that remote spot of Italy where the Vaudois had found an asylum. Petrarch first acquired a knowledge of the Greek tongue from Barlaam, a monk of Calabria; and Boccaccio was taught it from Leontius Pilatus, who was a hearer of Barlaam, if not also a native of the same place" [M'Crie, Italy, pp. 7,8]. Muston says that "the sciences flourished among them" [Muston, Israel of the Alps, p. 38]. The day of the Renaissance had not yet broken. The flight of scholars, which was to bear with it the seeds of ancient learning to the West, had not yet taken place; but the Vaudois of Calabria would seem to have anticipated that great literary revival. They had brought with them the Scriptures in the Romance version. They possessed doubtless the taste and genius for which the Romance nations were then famous; and, moreover, in their southern settlement they may have had access to some knowledge of those sciences which the Saracens then so assiduously cultivated; and what so likely, with their leisure and wealth, as that these Vaudois should turn their attention to letters as well as to husbandry, and make their adopted country vocal with the strains of that minstrelsy with which Provence and Dauphine had resounded so melodiously, till its music was quenched at once and for ever by the murderous arms of Simon de Montfort? But here we can only doubtfully guess, for the records of this interesting people are scanty and dubious.

These colonists kept up their connection with the mother country of the Valleys, though situated at the opposite extremity of Italy. To keep alive their faith, which was the connecting link, pastors were sent in relays of two to minister in the churches of Calabria and Apulia; and when they had fulfilled their term of two years they were replaced by other two. The barbes, on their way back to the Valleys, visited their brethren in the Italian towns; for at that time there were few cities in the peninsula in which the Vaudois were not to be found. The grandfather of the Vaudois historian, Gilles, in one of these pastoral visits to Venice, was assured by the Waldenses whom he there conversed with, that there were not fewer than 6,000 of their nation in that city. Fear had not yet awakened the suspicious and kindled the hatred of the Romanists, for the Reformation was not yet come. Nor did the Waldenses care to thrust their opinions upon the notice of their neighbors. Still the priests could not help observing that the manners of these northern settlers were, in many things, peculiar and strange. They eschewed revels and fetes; they had their children taught by foreign schoolmasters; in their churches was neither image nor lighted taper; they never went on pilgrimage; they buried their dead without the aid of the priests; and never were they known to bring a candle to the Virgin's shrine, or purchase a mass for the help of their dead relatives. These peculiarities were certainly startling, but one thing went far to atone for them-they paid with the utmost punctuality and fidelity their stipulated tithes; and as the value of their lands was yearly increasing, there was a corresponding yearly increase in both the tithe due to the priest and the rent payable the landlord, and neither was anxious to disturb a state of things so beneficial to himself, and which was every day becoming more advantageous [Perrin, Histoire des Vaudois, p. 197. Monastier, pp. 203-4].

But in the middle of the sixteenth century the breath of Protestantism from the North began to move over these colonies. The pastors who visited them told them of the synod which had been held in Angrogna in 1532, and which had been as the "beginning of months" to the ancient Church of the Valleys. More glorious tidings still did they communicate to the Christians of Calabria. In Germany, in France, in Switzerland, and in Denmark the old Gospel had blazed forth in a splendor unknown to it for ages. The Lamp of the Alps was no longer the one solitary light in the world: around it was a circle of mighty torches, whose rays, blending with those of the older luminary, were combining to dispel the night from Christendom. At the hearing of these stupendous things their spirit revived: their past conformity appeared to them like cowardice; they, too, would take part in the great work of the emancipation of the nations, by making open confession of the truth. No longer content with the mere visit of a pastor, they petitioned the mother Church to send them one who might permanently discharge amongst them the office of the holy minister.*

There was at that time a young minister at Geneva, a native of Italy, and him the Church of the Valleys designated to the perilous but honorable post. His name was Jean Louis Paschale; he was a native of Coni, in the Plain of Piedmont. By birth a Romanist, his first profession was that of arms; but from a knight of the sword he had become, like Loyola, through in a truer sense, a knight of the Cross. He had just completed his theological studies at Lausanne. He was betrothed to a young Piedmontese Protestant, Camilla Guerina [M'Crie, p. 324]. "Alas!" she sorrowfully exclaimed, when he intimated to her his departure for Calabria, "so near to Rome and so far from me." They parted, nevermore to meet on earth.

The young minister carried with him to Calabria the energetic spirit of Geneva. His preaching was with power; the zeal and courage of the Calabrian flock revived, and the light formerly hid under a bushel was now openly displayed. Its splendor attracted the ignorance and awoke the fanaticism of the region. The priests, who had tolerated a heresy that had conducted itself so modestly, and paid its dues so punctually, could be blind no longer. The Marquis of Spinello, who had been the protector of these colonists hitherto, finding his kindness more than repaid in the flourishing condition of his states, was compelled to move against them. "That

---

* Muston, p. 38. Monastier and M'Crie say that the application for a pastor was made to Geneva, and that Paschale set out for Calabria, accompanied by another minister and two schoolmasters. It is probable that the application was made to Geneva through the intermediation of the home Church.

dreadful thing, Lutheranism," he was told, "had broken in, and would soon destroy all things."

The marquis summoned the pastor and his flock before him. After a few moments' address from Paschale, the marquis dismissed the members of the congregation with a sharp reprimand, but the pastor he threw into the dungeons of Foscalda. The bishop of the diocese next took the matter into his own hands, and removed Paschale to the prison of Cosenza, where he was confined eight months.

The Pope heard of the case, and delegated Cardinal Alexandrini, Inquisitor-General, to extinguish the heresy in the Kingdom of Naples [Monastier, p. 205]. Alexandrini ordered Paschale to be removed from the Castle of Cosenza, and conducted to Naples. On the journey he was subjected to terrible sufferings. Chained to a gang of prisoners-the handcuffs so tight that they entered the flesh-he spent nine days on the road, sleeping at night on the bare earth, which was exchanged on his arrival at Naples for a deep, damp dungeon, the stench of which almost suffocated him [M'Crie, p. 325].

On the 16th of May, 1560, Paschale was taken in chains to Rome, and imprisoned in the Torre di Nona, where he was thrust into a cell not less noisome than that which he had occupied at Naples.

His brother, Bartolomeo, having obtained letters of recommendation, came from Coni to procure, if possible, some mitigation of his fate. The interview between the two brothers, as told by Bartolomeo, was most affecting. "It was quite hideous to see him," says he, "with his bare head, and his hands and arms lacerated by the small cords with which he was bound, like one about to be led to the gibbet. On advancing to embrace him I sank to the ground. 'My brother,' said he, 'if you are a Christian, why do you distress yourself thus? Do you know that a leaf cannot fall to the ground without the will of God? Comfort yourself in Christ Jesus, for the present troubles are not worthy to be compared with the glory to come.'" His brother, a Romanist, offered him half his fortune if only he would recant, and save his life. Even this token of affection could not move him. "Oh, my brother!" said he, "the danger in which you are involved gives me more distress than all that I suffer" [M'Crie, pp. 325-7].

He wrote to his affianced bride with a pen which, if it softened the picture of his own great sufferings, freely expressed the affection he bore for her, which "grows," says he, "with that I feel for God." Nor was he unmindful of his flock in Calabria. "My state is this," says he, in a letter which he addressed to them, "I feel my joy increase every day, as I approach nearer the hour in which I shall be offered a sweet-smelling sacrifice to the Lord Jesus Christ, my faithful Savior; yea, so inexpressible is my joy that I seem to myself to be free from captivity, and am prepared to die for Christ, and not only once, but ten thousand times, if it were possible; nevertheless, I persevere in imploring the Divine assistance by prayer, for I am convinced that man is a miserable creature when left to himself, and not upheld and directed by God" [Ibid., pp. 326-7].

CHAPTER 11
Extinction of Waldenses in Calabria

While Paschale was calmly awaiting a martyr's death in his dungeon at Rome, how fared it with his flock in Calabria, on whom the gathering storm had burst in terrific violence?

When it was known that Protestant ministers had been sent from Geneva to the Waldensian Churches in Calabria, the Inquisitor-General, as already mentioned, and two Dominican monks, Valerio Malvicino and Alfonso Urbino, were dispatched by the Sacred College to reduce these Churches to the obedience of the Papal See, or stamp them out. They arrived at San Sexto, and assembling the inhabitants, assured them it was not intended to do them any harm, would they but dismiss their Lutheran teachers and come to mass. The bell was rung for the celebration of the Sacrament, but the citizens instead of attending the service, left the town in a body, and retired to a neighboring wood. Concealing their chagrin, the inquisitors took their departure from San Sexto, and set out for La Guardia, the gates of which they locked behind them when they had entered, to prevent a second flight. Assembling the inhabitants, they told them that their co-religionists of San Sexto had renounced their errors, and dutifully attended mass, and they exhorted them to follow their good example, and return to the fold of the Roman shepherd; warning them at the same time, that should they refuse they would expose themselves, as heretics, to the loss of goods and life. The poor people, taken unawares, and believing what was told them, consented to hear mass; but no sooner was the ceremony ended, and the gates of the town opened, than they learned the deceit which had been practiced upon them. Indignant, and at the same time ashamed of their own weakness, they resolved to leave the place in a body, and join their brethren in the woods, but were withheld from their purpose by the persuasion and promises of their feudal superior, Spinello.

The Inquisitor-General, Alexandrini, now made request for two companies of men-at-arms, to enable him to execute his mission. The required aid was instantly given, and the soldiers were sent in pursuit of the inhabitants of San Sexto. Tracking them to their hiding-places, in the thickets and the caves of the mountains, they slaughtered many of them; others, who escaped, were pursued with bloodhounds, as if they had been wild beasts. Some of these fugitives scaled the craggy summits of the Apennines, and hurling down the stones on the soldiers who attempted to follow them, compelled them to desist from the pursuit.

Alexandrini dispatched a messenger to Naples for more troops to quell what he called the rebellion of the Vaudois. The viceroy obeyed the summons by coming in person with an army. He attempted to storm the fugitives, now strongly entrenched in the great mountains, whose summits of splintered rock, towering high above the pine forests that clothe their sides, presented to the fugitives an almost inaccessible retreat. The Waldenses offered to emigrate; but the viceroy would listen to nothing but their return within the pale of the Church of Rome. They were prepared to yield their lives rather than accept peace on such conditions. The viceroy now ordered his men to advance; but the shower of rocks that met his soldiers in the ascent hurled them to the bottom, a discomfited mass, in which maimed and dying were confusedly mingled with the corpses of the slain.

The viceroy, seeing the difficulty of the enterprise, issued an edict promising a free pardon to all bandits, outlaws, and other criminals who might be willing to undertake the task of scaling the mountains and attacking the strongholds of the Waldenses. In obedience to this summons, there assembled a mob of desperadoes, who were but too familiar with the secret paths of the Apennines. Threading their way through the woods, and clambering over the great rocks, these assassins rushed from every side on the barricades on the summit, and butchered the poor Vaudois. Thus were the inhabitants of San Sexto exterminated, some dying by the sword, some by fire, while others were torn by bloodhounds or perished by famine [Leger, part ii., p. 333. M'Crie, p. 303. Muston p. 41].

While the outlaws of the Neapolitan viceroy were busy in the mountains, the Inquisitor-General and his monks were pursuing their work of blood at La Guardia. The military force at their command not enabling them to take summary measures with the inhabitants, they had recourse to stratagem. Enticing the citizens outside the gates, and placing soldiers in ambush, they succeeded in getting into their power upwards of 1,600 persons [Monastier, p. 206]. Of these, seventy were sent in chains to Montalto, and tortured, in the hope of compelling them to accuse themselves of practicing shameful crimes in their religious assemblies. No such confession, however, could the most prolonged tortures wring from them. "Stefano Carlino," says M'Crie, "was tortured till his bowels gushed out;" and another prisoner, named Verminel, "was kept during eight hours on a horrid instrument called the hell, but persisted in denying the atrocious calumny" [M'Crie, p. 304]. Some were thrown from the tops of towers, or precipitated over cliffs; others were torn with iron whips, and finally beaten to death with fiery brands; and others, smeared with pitch, were burned alive.

But these horrors pale before the bloody tragedy at Montalto, enacted by the Marquis di Buccianici, whose zeal was quickened, it is said, by the promise of a cardinal's hat to his brother if he would clear Calabria of heresy. One's blood runs cold at the perusal of the deed. It was witnessed by a servant to Ascanio Caraccioli, himself a Roman Catholic, and described by him in a letter, which was published in Italy, along with other accounts of the horrible transaction, and has been quoted by M'Crie. "Most illustrious sir, I have now to inform you of the dreadful justice which began to be executed on these Lutherans early this morning, being the 11th of June. And, to tell you the truth, I can compare it to nothing but the slaughter of so many sheep. They were all shut up in one house as in a sheep-fold. The executioner went, and bringing out one of them, covered his face with a napkin, or benda, as we call it, led him out to a field near the house, and causing him to kneel down, cut his throat with a knife. Then, taking off the bloody napkin, he went and brought out another, whom he put to death after the same manner. In this way the whole number, amounting to eighty-eight men, were butchered. I leave you to figure to yourself the lamentable spectacle, for I can scarcely refrain from tears while I write; nor was there any person, after witnessing the execution of one, could stand to look on a second. The meekness and patience with which they went to martyrdom and death are incredible. Some of them at their death professed themselves of the same faith with us, but the greater part died in their cursed obstinacy. All the old met their death with cheerfulness, but the young exhibited symptoms of fear. I still shudder while I think of the executioner with the bloody knife in his teeth, the dripping napkin in his hand, and his arms besmeared with gore, going to the house, and taking out one victim after another, just as a butcher does the sheep which he means to kill" [Pantaleon, Rerum in Eccles. Gest. Hist., ff. 337-8. De Porta, tom. ii., pp. 309,312--ex M'Crie, pp. 305-6]. Their bodies were quartered, and stuck up on pikes along the high road leading from Montalto to Chateau-Vilar, a distance of thirty-six miles.

Numbers of men and women were burned alive, many were drafted off to the Spanish galleys, some made their submission to Rome, and a few, escaping from the scene of these horrors, reached, after infinite toil, their native Valleys, to tell that the once-flourishing Waldensian colony and Church in Calabria no longer existed, and that they only had been left to carry tidings to their brethren of its utter extermination.

Meanwhile, preparations had been made at Rome for the trial of Jean Louis Paschale. On the 8th of September, 1560, he was brought out of his prison, conducted to the Convent della Minerva, and cited before the Papal tribunal. He confessed his Savior, and, with a serenity to which the countenances of his judges were strangers, he listened to the sentence of death, which was carried into execution on the following day.

Standing upon the summit of the Janiculum Mount, vast crowds could witness the spectacle. In front the Campagna spreads out its once glorious but now desolated bosom; and winding through it like a thread of gold is seen the Tiber, while the Apennines, sweeping round it in craggy grandeur, enclose it like a vast wall. Immediately beneath, uprearing her domes and monuments and palaces, with an air that seems to say, "I sit a queen," is the city of Rome. Yonder, asserting an easy supremacy amid the other fabrics of the Eternal City, is the scarred and riven yet Titanic form of the Coliseum, with its stains of early Christian blood not yet washed out. By its side, the partner of its guilt and doom, lies the Palatine, once the palace of the world's master, now a low mound of ruins, with its row of melancholy cypresses, the only mourners on that site of vanished glory and fallen empire. Nearer, burning in the midday sun, is the proud cupola of St. Peter's, flanked on the one side by the buildings of the Inquisition, and on the other by the huge Mole of Hadrian, beneath whose gloomy ramparts old Tiber rolls sluggishly and sullenly along. But what shout is this which we hear? Why does Rome keep holiday? Why do all her bells ring? Lo! from every street and piazza eager crowds rush forth, and uniting in one overwhelming and surging stream, they are seen rolling across the Bridge of St. Angelo, and pressing in at the gates of the old fortress, which are thrown wide open to admit this mass of human beings.

Entering the court-yard of the old castle, an imposing sight meets the eye. What a confluence of ranks, dignities, and grandeurs! In the centre is placed a chair, the emblazonry of which tells us that it claims to rise in authority and dignity over the throne of kings. The Pontiff, Pius IV., has already taken his seat upon it, for he has determined to be present at the tragedy of to-day. Behind his chair, in scarlet robes, are his cardinals and counsellors, with many dignitaries besides in miters and cowls, ranged in circles, according to their place in the Papal body. Behind the ecclesiastics are seated, row on row, the nobility and beauty of Rome. Plumes wave, stars gleam, and seem to mock the frocks and cowls gathered near them, whose wearers, however, would not exchange these mystic garments for all the bravery that blazes around them. The vast sweep of the Court of St. Angelo is densely occupied. Its ample floor is covered from end to end with a closely-wedged mass of citizens, who have come to see the spectacle. In the centre of the throng, rising a little way over the sea of human heads, is seen a scaffold, with an iron stake, and beside it a bundle of faggots.

A slight movement begins to be perceptible in the crowd beside the gate. Some one is entering. The next moment a storm of hissing and execration salutes the ear. It is plain that the person who has just made his entrance is the object of universal dislike. The clank of irons on the stone floor of the court, as he comes forward, tells how heavily his limbs are loaded with fetters. He is still young; but his face is pale and haggard with suffering. He lifts his eyes, and with countenance undismayed surveys the vast assembly, and the dismal apparatus that stands in the midst of it, waiting its victim. There sits a calm courage on his brow; the serene light of deep, untroubled peace beams in his eye. He mounts the scaffold, and stands beside the stake. Every eye is now turned, not on the wearer of the tiara, but on the man who is clad in the sanbenito. "Good people," says the martyr-and the whole assembly keep silence-"I am come here to die for confessing the doctrine of my Divine Master and Savior, Jesus Christ." Then turning to Pius IV. he arraigned him as the enemy of Christ, the persecutor of his people, and the Anti-Christ of Scripture, and concluded by summoning him and all his cardinals to answer for their cruelties and murders before the throne of the Lamb. "At his words," says the historian Crespin, "the people were deeply moved, and the Pope and the cardinals gnashed their teeth."*

The inquisitors hastily gave the signal. The executioners came round him, and having strangled him, they kindled the faggots, and the flames blazing up speedily reduced his body to ashes. For once the Pope had performed his function. With his key of fire, which he may truly claim to carry, he had opened the celestial doors, and had sent his poor prisoner from the dark dungeons of the Inquisition, to dwell in the palace of the sky.

So died, or rather passed into the life eternal, Jean Louis Paschale, the Waldensian missionary and pastor of the flock in Calabria. His ashes were collected and thrown into the Tiber, and by the Tiber they were borne to the Mediterranean. And this was the grave of the preacher-martyr, whose noble bearing and undaunted courage before the Pope himself gave added value to his splendid testimony for the Protestant cause. Time may consume the marble, violence or war may drag down the monumental pile:

> "The pyramids that cleave heaven's jeweled portal;
> Elean Jove's star-spangled dome; the tomb
> Where rich Mausolus sleeps-are not immortal"
> [Sextus Propertius (Cranstoun's translation), p. 119].

But the tomb of the far-sounding sea to which the ashes of Paschale were committed, with a final display of impotent rage, was a nobler mausoleum than ever Rome raised to any of her Pontiffs.

---

* Crespin, Hist. des Martyrs, pp. 506-16. Leger, part i., p. 204, and part ii., p. 335.

CHAPTER 12
The Year of the Plague

A whole century nearly passed away between the trampling out of the Protestant Church in Calabria, and the next great persecution which befell that venerable people whose tragic history we are recording. We can touch only the more prominent of the events which fill up the interval.

The war the La Trinita, so ingloriously for himself, had waged against the Waldenses, ended, as we have seen, in a treaty of peace, which was signed at Cavour on the 5th of June, 1561, between Philip of Savoy and the deputies of the Valleys. But though the cloud had rolled past, it had left numerous and affecting memorials of the desolation it had inflicted. The inhabitants descended from the mountains to exchange the weapons of war for the spade and the pruning-knife. With steps slow and feeble the aged and the infirm were let down into the vales, to sit once more at noon or at eve beneath the shadow of their vines and ancestral chestnut-trees. But, alas! how often did the tear of sorrow moisten the eye as it marked the desolation and ruin that deformed those scenes lately so fair and smiling! The fruit-bearing trees cut down; vineyard and corn-field marred; hamlets burned; villages, in some cases, a heap of ruins, all testified to the rage of the enemy who had invaded their land. Years must pass before these deep scars could be effaced, and the beauty of their Valleys restored. And there were yet tender griefs weighing upon them. How many were there who had lived under the same roof-tree with them, and joined night and morning in the same psalm, who would return no more!

Distress, bordering on famine, began to invade the Valleys. Seven months of incessant fighting had left them no time to cultivate the fields; and now the stock of last year's provisions was exhausted, and starvation stared them in the face. Before the treaty of peace was signed, the time of sowing was past, and when the autumn came there was scarcely anything to reap. Their destitution was further aggravated by the fugitives from Calabria, who began about this time to arrive in the Valleys. Escaping with nothing but their lives, they presented themselves in hunger and nakedness. Their brethren opened their arms to receive them, and though their own necessities were great, they nevertheless shared with them the little they had.

The tale of the suffering now prevailing in the Valleys was known in other countries, and evoked the sympathy of their Protestant brethren. Calvin, with characteristic promptness and ardor, led in the movement for their relief. By his advice they sent deputies to represent their case to the Churches of Protestantism abroad, and collections were made for them in Geneva, France, Switzerland, and Germany. The subscriptions were headed by the Elector Palatine, after whom came the Duke of Wurtemburg, the Canton of Bern, the Church at Strasburg, and others.

By-and-by, seed-time and harvest were restored in the Valleys; smiling chalets began again to dot the sides of their mountains, and to rise by the banks of their torrents; and the miseries which La Trinita's campaign had entailed upon them were passing into oblivion, when their vexations were renewed by the appointment of a deputy-governor of their Valleys, Castrocaro, a Tuscan by birth.

This man had served against the Vaudois as a colonel of militia under La Trinita; he had been taken prisoner in an encounter with them, but honorably treated, and at length generously released. He returned the Waldenses evil for good. His appointment as Governor of the Valleys he owed mainly to his acquaintance with the Duchess Margaret, the protectress of the Vaudois, into whose favor he had ingratiated himself by professing a warm affection for the men of the Valleys; and his friendship with the Archibishop of Turin, to whom he had pledged himself to do his utmost to convert the Vaudois to Romanism. When at length Castrocaro arrived in the Valleys in the character of governor, he forgot his professions to the duchess, but faithfully set about fulfilling the promise he had made to the archbishop.

The new governor began by restricting the liberties guaranteed to their Churches in the treaty of peace; he next ordered the dismissal of certain pastors, and when their congregations refused to comply, he began to fine and imprison the recusants. He sent false and calumnious reports to the court of the duke, and introduced a troop of soldiers into the country, on the pretext that the Waldenses were breaking out into rebellion. He built the fortress of Miraboue, at the foot of the Col de la Croix, in the narrow gorge that leads from Bobbio to France, to close this gate of exit from their territory, and overawe the Valley of Lucerna. At last he threatened to renew the war unless the Waldenses should comply with his wishes.

What was to be done? They carried their complaints and remonstrances to Turin; but, alas! the ear of the duke and duchess had been poisoned by the malice and craft of the governor. Soon again the old alternative would be presented to them, the mass or death [Muston, chap. 16. Monastier, chap. 21].

In their extremity they sought the help of the Protestant princes of Germany. The cry from the Alps found a responsive echo from the German plains. The great Protestant chiefs of the Fatherland, especially Frederick, Elector Palatine, saw in these poor oppressed herdsmen and vine-dressers his brethren, and with zeal and warmth espoused their cause. He indicted a letter to the duke, distinguished for its elevation of sentiment, as well as the catholicity of its views. It is a noble defense of the rights of conscience, and an eloquent pleading in behalf of toleration. "Let your highness," says the Elector, "know that there is a God in heaven, who not only contemplates the actions, but also tries the hearts and reigns of men, and from whom nothing is hid. Let your highness take care not voluntarily to make war upon God, and not to persecute Christ in his members. ...Persecution, moreover, will never advance the cause it pretends to defend. The ashes of the martyrs are the seed of the Christian Church. For the church resembles the palm-tree, whose stem only shoots up the taller the greater the weights that are hung upon it. Let your highness consider that the Christian religion was established by persuasion, and not by violence; and as it is certain that religion is nothing else than a firm and enlightened persuasion of God, and of his will, as revealed in his Word, and engraven in the hearts of believers by his Holy Spirit, it cannot, when once rooted, be torn away by tortures" [see the letter in full in Leger, part i., pp. 41-5]. So did the Elector Palatine warn the duke.

These are remarkable words when we think that they were written in the middle of the sixteenth century. We question whether our own age could express itself more justly on the subject of the rights of conscience, the spirituality of religion, and the impolicy, as well as criminality, of persecution. We sometimes apoligize for the cruel deeds of Spain and France, on the ground of the intolerance and blindness of the age. But six years before the St. Bartholomew Massacre was enacted, this great voice had been raised in Christendom for toleration.

What effect this letter had upon the duke we do not certainly know, but from about this time Castrocaro moderated his violence, though he still continued at intervals to terrify the poor people he so basely oppressed by fulminating against them the most atrocious threats. On the death of Emanuel Philibert, in 1580, the villainy of the governor came to light. The young Duke Charles Emanuel ordered his arrest; but the execution of it was a matter of difficulty, for Castrocaro had entrenched himself in the Castle of La Torre, and surrounded himself with a band of desperadoes, to which he had added, for his yet greater defense, a pack of ferocious bloodhounds of unusual size and strength [Muston, p. 98]. A captain of his guard betrayed him, and thus as he had maintained himself by treachery, so by treachery did his doom at last overtake him. He was carried to Turin, where he perished in prison [Monastier, p. 222].

Famine, persecution, war-all three, sometimes in succession and sometimes together-had afflicted this much-enduring people, but now they were to be visited by pestilence. For some years they had enjoyed an unusual peace; and this quiet was the more remarkable inasmuch as all around their mountains Europe was in combustion. Their brethren of the Reformed Church in France, in Spain, and in Italy were falling on the field, perishing by massacre, or dying at the stake, while they were guarded from harm. But now a new calamity carried gloom and mourning into their Valleys. On the morning of the 23rd of August, 1629, a cloud of unusual blackness gathered on the summit of the Cod Julien. It burst in a water-spout or deluge. The torrents rolled down the mountain on both sides, and the villages of Bobbio and Prali, situated the one in the southern and the other in the northern valley, were overflown by the sudden inundation. Many of the houses were swept away, and the inhabitants had barely time to save their lives by flight. In September of the same year, there came an icy wind, accompanied by a dry cloud, which scathed their Valleys and destroyed the crop of the chestnut-tree. There followed a second deluge of rain, which completely ruined the vintage. These calamities were the more grievous inasmuch as they succeeded a year of partial famine. The Vaudois pastors assembled in solemn synod, to humble themselves and to lift up their voices in prayer to God. Little did they imagine that at that moment a still heavier calamity hung over them, and that this was the last time they were ever to meet one another on earth [Muston, p. 111].

In 1630, a French army, under Marshal Schomberg, suddenly occupied the Valleys. In that army were many volunteers, who had made their escape from a virulent contagious disease then raging in France. The weather was hot, and the seeds of the pestilence which the army had brought with it speedily developed themselves. The plague showed itself in the first week of May in the Valley of Perosa; it next broke out in the more northern Valley of San Martino; and soon it spread throughout all the Valleys. The pastors met together to supplicate the Almighty, and to concert practical measures for checking the ravages of this mysterious and terrible scourge. They purchased medicine and collected provisions for the poor [Monastier, p. 241]. They visited the sick, consoled the dying, and preached in the open air to crowds, solemnized and eager to listen.

In July and August the heat was excessive, and the malady raged yet more furiously. In the month of July four of the pastors were carried off by the plague; in August seven others died; and in the following month another, the twelfth, was mortally stricken. There remained now only three pastors, and it was remarked that they belonged to three several valleys-Lucerna, Martino, and Perosa. The three survivors met on the heights of Angrogna, to consult with the deputies of the various parishes regarding the means of providing for the celebration of worship. They wrote to Geneva and Dauphine requesting that pastors might be sent to supply the place of those whom the plague had struck down, that so the venerable Church of the Valleys, which had survived so many calamities, might not become extinct. They also recalled Antoine Leger from Constantinople [Muston, pp. 112-3. Antoine Leger was uncle of Leger the historian. He had been tutor for many years in the family of the Ambassador of Holland at Constantinople].

The plague subsided during the winter, but in spring (1631) it rose up again in renewed force. Of the three surviving pastors, one other died; leaving thus only two, Pierre Gilles of Lucerna, and Valerius Gross of Martino. With the heats of the summer the pestilence waxed in strength. Armies, going and coming in the Valleys, suffered equally with the inhabitants. Horsemen would be seen to drop from the saddle on the highway, seized with sudden illness. Soldiers and sutlers, struck in by-paths, lay there infecting the air with their corpses. In La Torre alone fifty families became extinct. The most moderate estimate of the numbers cut off by the plague is 10,000, or from a half to two-thirds of the entire population of the Valleys. The corn in many places remained uncut, the grapes rotted in many places remained uncut, the grapes rotted on the bough, and the fruit dropped from the tree. Strangers who had come to find health in the pure mountain air obtained from the soil nothing but a grave. Towns and villages, which had rung so recently from the sounds of industry, were now silent. Parents were without children, and children were without parents. Patriarchs, who had been wont with pride and joy to gather round them their numerous grandchildren, had seen them sicken and die, and were now alone. The venerable pastor Gilles lost his four elder sons. Though continually present in the homes of the stricken, and at the bedsides of the dying, he himself was spared to compile the monuments of his ancient Church, and narrate among other woes that which had just passed over his native land, and "part of which he had been."

Of the Vaudois pastors only two now remained; and ministers hastened from Geneva and other places to the Valleys, lest the old lamp should go out. The services of the Waldensian Churches had hitherto been performed in the Italian tongue, but the new pastors could speak only French. Worship was henceforward conducted in that language, but the Vaudois soon came to understand it, their own ancient tongue being a dialect between the French and Italian. Another change introduced at this time was the assimilation of their ritual to that of Geneva. And further, the primitive and affectionate name of Barba was dropped, and the modern title substituted, Monsieur le Ministre [Monastier, chap. 18. Muston, pp. 242-3].

CHAPTER 13
The Great Massacre

The first labor of the Waldenses, on the departure of the plague, was the re-organization of society. There was not a house in all their Valleys where death had not been; all ties had been rent, the family was all but extinct; but now, the destroyer being gone, the scattered inhabitants began to draw together, and to join hand and heart in restoring the ruined churches, raising up the fallen habitations, and creating anew family and home.

Other events of an auspicious kind, which occurred at this time, contributed to revive the spirits of the Waldenses, and to brighten with a gleam of hope the scene of the recent great catastrophe. The army took its departure, peace having been signed between the French monarch and the duke, and the Valleys returned once more under the dominion of the House of Savoy. A decade and a half of comparative tranquility allowed the population to root itself anew, and their Valleys and mountain-sides to be brought again under tillage. Fifteen years-how short a breathing-space amid storms so awful!

These fifteen years draw to a close; it is now 1650, and the Vaudois are entering within the shadow of their greatest woe. The throne of Savoy was at this time filled by Charles Emmanuel II, a youth of fifteen. He was a prince of mild and humane disposition; but he was counseled and ruled by his mother, the Duchess Christina, who had been appointed regent of the kingdom during his minority. That mother was sprung of a race which has ever been noted for its dissimulation, its cruelty, and its bigoted devotion to Rome. She was the daughter of Henry IV. and Mary de Medici, and granddaughter of that Catherine de Medici whose name stands

112

so conspicuously connected with a tragedy which has received, as it merited, the execration of mankind-the St. Bartholomew Massacre. The ferocious temper and gloomy superstition of the grandmother had descended to the granddaughter. In no reign did the tears and blood of the Waldenses flow so profusely, a fact for which we cannot satisfactorily account, unless on the supposition that the sufferings which now overwhelmed them came not from the mild prince who occupied the throne, but from the cold, cruel, and bloodthirsty regent who governed the kingdom. In short, there is reason to believe that it was not the facile spirit of the House of Savoy, but the astute spirit of the Medici, prompted by the Vatican, that enacted those scenes of carnage that we are now to record.

The blow did not descend all at once; a series of lesser attacks heralded the great and consummating stroke. Machinations, chicaneries, and legal robberies paved the way for an extermination that was meant to be complete and final.

First of all came the monks. Pestilence, as we have seen, visited the Valleys in 1630. There came, however, a second plague-not this time the pestilence, but a swarm of Capuchins. They had been sent to convert the heretics, and they began by eagerly challenging the pastors to a controversy, in which they felt sure of triumphing. A few attempts, however, convinced them that victory was not to be so easily won as they had fondly thought. The heretics made "a Pope of their Bible," they complained, and as this was a book which the Fathers had not studied, they did not know where to find the passages which they were sure would confute the Vaudois pastors; they could silence them only by banishing them, and among others whom they drove into exile was the accomplished Antoine Leger, the uncle of the historian. Thus were the people deprived of their natural leaders [Muston, p. 126]. The Vaudois were forbidden on pain of confiscation and death to purchase or farm lands outside their own narrow territories. Certain of their churches were closed. Their territory was converted into a prison by an order forbidding them to cross the frontier even for a few hours, unless on fair-days. The wholly Protestant communes of Bobbio, Villaro, Angrogna, and Rora were ordered to maintain each a mission of Capuchins; and foreign Protestants were interdicted from settling in the Valleys under pain of death, and a fine of 1,000 gold crowns upon the communes that should receive them. This law was leveled against their pastors, who, since the plague, were mostly French or Swiss. It was hoped that in a few years the Vaudois would be without ministers. Monts-de-Piete were established to induce the Vaudois, whom confiscations, bad harvests, and the billeting of soldiers had reduced to great straits, to pawn their goods, and when all had been put in pledge they were offered restitution in full on condition of renouncing their faith. Dowries were promised to young maidens on the same terms [Muston, p. 129]. These various arts had a success surprisingly small. Some dozen of Waldensian perverts were added to the Roman Church. It was plain that the good work of proselytizing was proceeding too slowly. More efficient measures must be had recourse to.

The Society for the "Propagation of the Faith," established by Pope Gregory XV in 1622, had already been spread over Italy and France. The object of the society was originally set forth in words sufficiently simple and innocent-"De Propaganda Fide" (for the Propagation of the Faith). Since the first institution of this society, however, its object had undergone enlargement, or, if not its object, at all events its title. Its first modern designation was supplemented by the emphatic words, "et Extirpandis Haereticis" (and the Extirpation of Heretics). The membership of the society soon became numerous: it included both laymen and priests; all ranks, from the noble and the prelate to the peasant and the pauper, pressed forward to enroll themselves in it-the inducement being a plenary indulgence to all who should take part in the good work so unmistakably indicated in the one brief and pithy clause, "et Extirpandis Haereticis." The societies in the smaller towns reported to the metropolitan cities; the metropolitan cities to the capital; and the capitals to Rome, where, in the words of Leger, "sat the great spider that held the threads of this mighty web."

In 1650 the "Council of the Propagation of the Faith" was established at Turin. The chief councilors of state, the great lords of the country, and the dignitaries of the Church enrolled themselves as a presiding board. Societies of women were formed, at the head of which was the Marchioness de Pianeza. She was the first lady at court; and as she had not worn "the white rose of a blameless life," she was all the more zealous in this cause, in the hope of making expiation for the errors of the past. She was at infinite pains to further the object of the society; and her own eager spirit she infused into all under her. "The lady propagandists," says Leger

[Leger, part ii., chap. 6, pp. 72-3], "distributed the towns into districts, and each visited the district assigned to her twice a week, suborning simple girls, servant maids, and young children by their flattering allurements and fair promises, and doing evil turns to such as would not listen to them. They had their spies everywhere, who, among other information, ascertained in what Protestant families disagreement existed, and hither would the propagandists repair, stirring up the flame of dissension in order to separate the husband, the children from the parents; promising them, and indeed giving them, great advantages, if they would consent to attend mass. Did they hear of a tradesman whose business was falling off, or of a gentleman who from gambling or otherwise was in want of money, those ladies were at hand with their Dabo tibi (I will give thee), on condition of apostasy; and the prisoner was in like manner relieved from his dungeon, who would give himself up to them. To meet the very heavy expenses of this proselytizing, to keep the machinery at work, to purchase the souls that sold themselves for bread, regular collections were made in the chapels, and in private families, in the shops, in the inns, in the gambling-houses, in the streets-everywhere was alms-begging in operation. The Marchioness of Pianeza herself, great lady as she was, used every second or third day to make a circuit in search of subscriptions, even going into the taverns for that purpose ... If any person of condition, who was believed able to contribute a coin, chanced to arrive at any hotel in town, these ladies did not fail to wait upon him, purse in hand, and solicit a donation. When persons of substance known to belong to the religion [Reformed] arrived in Turin, they did not scruple to ask money of them for the propagation of the faith, and the influence of the marchioness, or fear of losing their errand and ruining their affairs, would often induce such to comply."

While busied in the prosecution of these schemes the Marchioness de Pianeza was stricken with death. Feeling remorse, and wishing to make atonement, she summoned her lord, from whom she had been parted many years, to her bedside, and charged him, as he valued the repose of her soul and the safety of his own, to continue the good work, on which her heart had been so much set, of converting the Vaudois. To stimulate his zeal, she bequeathed him a sum of money, which, however, he could not touch till he had fulfilled the condition on which it was granted. The marquis undertook the task with the utmost goodwill [Muston, p. 130]. A bigot and a soldier, he could think of only one way of converting the Vaudois. It was now that the storm burst.

On the 25th of January, 1655, came the famous order of Gastaldo. This decree commanded all the Vaudois families domiciled in the communes of Lucerna, Fenile, Bubiana, Bricherasio, San Giovanni, and La Torre-in short, the whole of that rich district that separates their capital from the plain of Piedmont-to quit their dwellings within three days, and retire into the Valleys of Bobbio, Angrogna, and Rora. This they were to do on pain of death. They were further required to sell their lands to Romanists within twenty days. Those who were willing to abjure the Protestant faith were exempted from the decree.

Anything more inhuman and barbarous under the circumstances than this edict it would not be easy to imagine. It was the depth of winter, and an Alpine winter has terrors unknown to the winters of even more northern regions. How ever could a population like that on which the decree fell, including young children and old men, the sick and bed-ridden, the blind and the lame, undertake a journey across swollen rivers, through valleys buried in snow, and over mountains covered with ice? They must inevitably perish, and the edict that cast them out was but another form of condemning them to die of cold and hunger. "Pray ye," said Christ, when warning his disciples to flee when they should see the Roman armies gathering round Jerusalem, "pray ye that your flight be not in the winter." The Romish Propaganda at Turin chose this season for the enforced flight of the Vaudois. Cold were the icy peaks that looked down on this miserable troop, who were now fording the torrents and now struggling up the mountain tracks; but the heart of the persecutor was colder still. True, an alternative was offered them; they might go to mass. Did they avail themselves of it? The historian Leger informs us that he had a congregation of well-nigh 2,000 persons, and that not a man of them all accepted the alternative. "I can well bear them this testimony," he observes, "seeing I was their pastor for eleven years, and I knew every one of them by name; judge, reader, whether I had not cause to weep for joy, as well as for sorrow, when I saw that all the fury of these wolves was not able to influence one of these lambs, and that no earthly advantage could shake their constancy. And when I marked the traces of their blood on the snow and ice over which they had dragged their lacerated limbs, had I not cause to bless God that I had seen accomplished in their poor bodies what remained of the measure of the sufferings of Christ, and especially when I beheld this heavy cross borne by them with a fortitude so noble?" [Leger, part. ii., chap. 8, p. 94].

The Vaudois of the other valleys welcomed these poor exiles, and joyfully shared with them their own humble and scanty fare. They spread the table for all, and loaded it with polenta and roasted chestnuts, with the milk and butter of their mountains, to which they did not forget to add a cup of that red wine which their valleys produce [Monastier, p. 265]. Their enemies were amazed when they saw the whole community rise up as one man and depart.

Greater woes trod fast upon the heels of this initial calamity. A part only of the Vaudois nation had suffered from the cruel decree of Gastaldo; but the fixed object of the Propaganda was the extirpation of the entire race, and the matter was gone about with consummate perfidy and deliberate cruelty. From the upper valleys, to which they had retired, the Waldenses sent respectful representations to the court of Turin. They described their piteous condition in terms so moving–and it would have been hard to have exaggerated it–and besought the fulfillment of treaties in which the honor and truth of the House of Savoy were pledged, in language so temperate and just, that one would have thought that their supplication must needs prevail. Alas, no! The ear of their prince had been poisoned by false-hood. Even access to him was denied them. As regarded the Propaganda, their remonstrances, though accompanied with tears and groans, were wholly unheeded. The Vaudois were but charming deaf adders. They were put off with equivocal answers and delusive promises till the fatal 17th of April had arrived, when it was no longer necessary to dissemble and equivocate [Leger, part ii., pp. 95-6].

On the day above named, April 17th, 1655, the Marquis de Pianeza departed secretly at midnight from Turin, and appeared before the Valleys at the head of an army of 15,000 men [Ibid, part iv., p. 108]. Waldensian deputies were by appointment knocking at the door of the marquis in Turin, while he himself was on the road to La Torre, He appeared under the walls of that town at eight o'clock on Saturday evening, the same 17th of April, attended by about 300 men; the main body of his army he had left encamped on the plain. That army, secretly prepared, was composed of Piedmontese, comprising a good many banditti, who were promised pardon and plunder should they behave themselves well, some companies of Bavarians, six regiments of French, whose thirst for blood the Huguenot wars had not been able to slake, and several companies of Irish Romanists, who, banished by Cromwell, arrived in Piedmont dripping from the massacre of their Protestant fellow-subjects in their native land [Monastier, p. 267].

The Waldenses had hastily constructed a barricade at the entrance of La Torre. The marquis ordered his soldiers to storm it; but the besieged resisted so stoutly that, after three hours' fighting, the enemy found he had made no advance. At one o'clock on the Sunday morning, Count Amadeus of Lucerna, who knew the locality, made a flank movement along the banks of the Pelice, stole silently through the meadows and orchards, and, advancing from the opposite quarter, attacked the Vaudois in the rear. They faced round, pierced the ranks of their assailants, and made good their retreat to the hills, leaving La Torre in the hands of the enemy. The Vaudois had lost only three men in all that fighting. It was now between two and three o'clock on Sunday morning, and though the hour was early, the Romanists repaired in a body to the church and chanted a Te Deum [Muston, p. 135]. The day was Palm-Sunday, and in this fashion did the Roman Church, by her soldiers, celebrate that great festival of love and goodwill in the Waldensian Valleys.

The Vaudois were once more on their mountains. Their families had been previously transported to their natural fastnesses. Their sentinels kept watch night and day along the frontier heights. They could see the movements of Pianeza's army on the plains beneath. They beheld their orchards falling by the axes, and their dwellings being consumed by the torches of the soldiers. On Monday the 19th, and Tuesday the 20th, a series of skirmishes took place along the line of their mountain passes and forts. The Vaudois, though poorly armed and vastly outnumbered-for they were but as one to a hundred-were victorious on all points. The Popish soldiers fell back in ignominious rout, carrying wondrous tales of the Vaudois' valor and heroism to their comrades on the plain, and infusing incipient panic into the camp [Leger, part ii., pp. 108-9].

Guilt is ever cowardly. Pianeza now began to have misgivings touching the issue. The recollection that mighty armies had aforetime perished on these mountains haunted and disquieted him. He betook him to a weapon which the Waldenses have ever been less able to cope with than the sword. On Wednesday, the 21st, before daybreak, he announced, by sound of trumpet at the various Vaudois entrenchments, his willingness to receive their deputies and treat for peace. Delegates set out for his camp, and on their arrival at head-quarters were received with the utmost urbanity, and sumptuously entertained. Pianeza expressed the utmost regret for the excesses his soldiers had committed, and which had been done, he said, contrary to orders. He protested that he had come into their valleys only to track a few fugitives who had disobeyed Gastaldo's order, that the higher communes had nothing to fear, and that if they would admit a single regiment each for a few days, in token of their loyalty, all would be amicably ended. The craft of the man conquered the deputies, and despite the warnings of the more sagacious, the pastor Leger in particular, the Waldenses opened the passes of their valleys and the doors of their dwellings to the soldiers of Pianeza.

Alas! alas! these poor people were undone. They had received under their roof the murderers of themselves and their families. The first two days, the 22nd and 23rd of April, were passed in comparative peace, the soldiers eating at the same table, sleeping under the same roof, and conversing freely with their destined victims. This interval was needed to allow every preparation to be made for what was to follow. The enemy now occupied the towns, the villages, the cottages, and the roads throughout the valleys. They hung upon the heights. Two great passes led into France: the one over the snows of the lofty Col Julien, and the other by the Valley of Queyras into Dauphine. But, alas! escape was not possible by either outlet. No one could traverse the Col Julien at this season and live, and the fortress of Miraboue, that guarded the narrow gorge which led into the Valley of Queyras, the enemy had been careful to secure [Leger, part ii., p. 110]. The Vaudois were enclosed as in a net-shut in as in a prison.

At last the blow fell with the sudden crash of the thunderbolt. At four o'clock on the morning of Saturday, the 24th of April, 1655, the signal was given from the castle-hill of La Torre. [So says Leger, who was an eye-witness of these horrors]. But who shall rehearse the tragedy that followed? "It is Cain a second time," says

Monastier, "shedding the blood of his brother Abel" [Monastier, p. 270]. On the instant a thousand assassins began the work of death. Dismay, horror, agony, woe in a moment overspread the Valleys of Lucerna and Angrogna. Though Pandemonium had sent forth its fiends to riot in crime and revel in blood, they could not have outdone the soldiers of the Propaganda. Though the victims climbed the hills with what speed they could, the murderer was on their track. The torrents as they rolled down from the heights soon began to be tinged with blood. Gleams of lurid light burst out through the dark smoke that was rolling through the vales, for a priest and monk accompanied each party of soldiers, to set fire to the houses as soon as the inmates had been dispatched. Alas! what sounds are those that repeatedly strike the ear? The cries and groans of the dying were echoed and re-echoed from the rocks around, and it seemed as if the mountains had taken up a wailing for the slaughter of their children. "Our Valley of Lucerna," exclaims Leger, "which was like a Goshen, was now converted into a Mount Etna, darting forth cinders and fire and flames. The earth resembled a furnace, and the air was filled with a darkness like that of Egypt, which might be felt, from the smoke of towns, villages, temples, mansions, granges, and buildings, all burning in the flames of the Vatican" [Leger, part ii., p. 113].

The soldiers were not content with the quick dispatch of the sword, they invented new and hitherto unheard-of modes of torture and death. No man at this day dare write in plain words all the disgusting and horrible deeds of these men; their wickedness can never be all known, because it never can be all told.

From the awful narration of Leger, we select only a few instances; but even these few, however mildly stated, grow, without our intending it, into a group of horrors. Little children were torn from the arms of their mothers, clasped by their tiny feet, and their heads dashed against the rocks; or were held between two soldiers and their quivering limbs torn up by main force. Their mangled bodies were then thrown on the highways or fields, to be devoured by beasts. The sick and the aged were burned alive in their dwellings. Some had their hands and arms and legs lopped off, and fire applied to the severed parts to staunch the bleeding and prolong their suffering. Some were flayed alive, some were roasted alive, some disemboweled; or tied to trees in their own orchards, and their hearts cut out. Some were horribly mutilated, and of others the brains were boiled and eaten by these cannibals. Some were fastened down into the furrows of their own fields, and ploughed into the soil as men plough manure into it. Others were buried alive. Fathers were marched to death with the heads of their sons suspended round their necks. Parents were compelled to look on while their children were first outraged, then massacred, before being themselves permitted to die. But here we must stop. We cannot proceed farther in Leger's awful narration. There come vile, abominable, and monstrous deeds, utterly and overwhelmingly disgusting, horrible and fiendish, which we dare not transcribe. The heart sickens, and the brain begins to swim. "My hand trembles," says Leger, "so that I scarce can hold the pen, and my tears mingle in torrents with my ink, while I write the deeds of these children of darkness-blacker even than the Prince of Darkness himself" [Leger, part ii., p. 111].

No general account, however awful, can convey so correct an idea of the horrors of this persecution as would the history of individual cases; but this we are precluded from giving. Could we take these martyrs one by one-could we describe the tragical fate of Peter Simeon of Angrogna-the barbarous death of Magdalene, wife of Peter Pilon of Villaro-the sad story-but no, that story could not be told-of Anne, daughter of John Charbonier of La Torre-the cruel martyrdom of Paul Garnier of Rora, whose eyes were first plucked out, who next endured other horrible indignities, and, last of all, was flayed alive, and his skin, divided into four parts, extended on the window gratings of the four principal houses in Lucerna-could we describe these cases, with hundreds of others equally horrible and appalling, our narrative would grow so harrowing that our readers, unable to proceed, would turn from the page. Literally did the Waldenses suffer all the things of which the apostle speaks, as endured by the martyrs of old, with other torments not then invented, or which the rage of even a Nero shrank from inflicting:--"They were stoned, they were sawn asunder, were tempted, were slain with the sword; they wandered about in sheep-skins and goat-skins; being destitute, afflicted, tormented (of whom the world was not worthy); they wandered in deserts, and in mountains, and in dens, and caves of the earth."

These cruelties form a scene that is unparalleled and unique in the history of at least civilized countries. There have been tragedies in which more blood was spilt and more life sacrificed, but none in which the actors were so completely dehumanized, and the forms of suffering so monstrously disgusting, so unutterably cruel and revolting. The Piedmontese Massacres in this respect stand alone. They are more fiendish than all the atrocities and murders before or since, and Leger may still advance his challenge to "all travelers, and all who have studied the history of ancient and modern pagans, whether among the Chinese, Tartars and Turks, they ever witnessed or heard tell of such execrable perfidies and barbarities."

The authors of these deeds, thinking it may be that their very atrocity would make the world slow to believe them, made bold to deny that they had ever been done, even before the blood was well dry in the Valleys. Pastor Leger took instant and effectual means to demonstrate the falsehood of that denial, and to provide that clear, irrefragable, and indubitable proof of these awful crimes should go down to posterity. He traveled from commune to commune, immediately after the massacre, attended by notaries, who took down the depositions and attestations of the survivors and eye-witnesses of these deeds, in presence of the council and consistory of the place [Leger, part ii., p. 112]. From the evidence of these witnesses he compiled and gave to the world a book, which Dr. Gilly truly characterized as one of the most "dreadful" in existence. [The book is that from which we have so largely quoted, entitled Histoire Generale des Eglises Evangeliques des Vallees de Piemont ou Vaudoises. Par Jean Leger, Pasteur et Moderateur des Eglises des Vallees, et depuis la violence de la Persecution, appele a l'Eglise Wallonne de Leyde. A. Leyde, 1669.] The originals of these depositions Leger gave to Sir Samuel Morland, who deposited them, together with other valuable documents pertaining to the Waldenses, in the Library of the University of Cambridge.

Uncontrollable grief seized the hearts of the survivors at the sight of their brethren slain, their country devastated, and their Church overthrown. "Oh that my head were waters," exclaims Leger, "and mine eyes a fountain of tears, that I might weep day and night for the slain of the daughter of my people! Behold and see if there be any sorrow like unto my sorrow." "It was then," he adds, "that the fugitives, who had been snatched as brands from the burning, could address God in the words of the 79th Psalm, which literally as emphatically describes their condition:--

"'O God, the heathen are come into thine inheritance,
  Thy holy temple have they defiled;

> They have laid Jerusalem on heaps.
> The dead bodies of thy servants have they given
> To be meat unto the fowls of heaven,
> The flesh of thy saints unto the beasts of the earth,
> Their blood have they shed like water;...
> And there was none to bury them!"
> [Leger, part ii., p. 113].

When the storm had abated, Leger assembled the scattered survivors, in order to take counsel with them as to the steps to be now taken. It does not surprise us to find that some had begun to entertain the idea of abandoning the Valleys altogether. Leger strongly dissuaded them against the thought of forsaking their ancient inheritance. They must, he said, rebuild their Zion in the faith that the God of their fathers would not permit the Church of the Valleys to be finally overthrown. To encourage them, he undertook to lay a representation of their sufferings and broken condition before their brethren of other countries, who, he was sure, would hasten to their help at this great crisis. These counsels prevailed. "Our tears are no longer of water," so wrote the remnant of the slaughtered Vaudois to the Protestants of Europe, "they are of blood; they do not merely obscure our sight, they choke our very hearts. Our hands tremble and our heads ache by the many blows we have received. We cannot frame an epistle answerable to the intent of our minds, and the strangeness of our desolations. We pray you to excuse us, and to collect amid our groans the meaning of what we fain would utter." After this touching introduction, they proceeded with a representation of their state, expressing themselves in terms the moderation of which contrasts strongly with the extent of their wrongs. Protestant Europe was horror-struck when it heard of the massacre.

Nowhere did these awful tidings awaken a deeper sympathy or kindle a stronger indignation than in England. Cromwell, who was then at the head of the State, proclaimed a fast, ordered a collection for the sufferers, and wrote to all the Protestant princes, and to the King of France, with the intent of enlisting their sympathy and aid in behalf of the Vaudois. [The sum collected in England was, in round numbers, 38,000 pounds. Of this, 16,000 pounds was invested, on the security of the State, to pension pastors, schoolmasters, and students in the Valleys. This latter sum was appropriated by Charles II, on the pretext that he was not bound to implement the engagements of a usurper. One of the noblest as well as most sacred of the tasks ever undertaken by the great poet, who then acted as the Protector's Latin secretary, was the writing of these letters. Milton's pen was not less gloriously occupied when writing in behalf of these venerable sufferers for conscience's sake, than when writing "Paradise Lost." In token of the deep interest he took in this affair, Cromwell sent Sir Samuel Morland with a letter to the Duke of Savoy, expressive of the astonishment and sorrow he felt at the barbarities which had been committed on those who were his brethren in the faith. Cromwell's ambassador visited the Valleys on his way to Turin, and saw with his own eyes the frightful spectacle which the region still presented. "If," said he, addressing the duke, the horrors he had just seen giving point to his eloquence, and kindling his republican plainness into Puritan fervor, "If the tyrants of all times and ages were alive again, they would doubtless be ashamed to find that nothing barbarous nor inhuman, in comparison of these deeds, had ever been invented by them. In the meantime," he continued, "the angels are stricken with horror; men are dizzy with amazement; heaven itself appears astonished with the cries of the dying, and the very earth to blush with the gore of so many innocent persons. Avenge not thyself, O God, for this mighty wickedness, this parricidal slaughter! Let they blood, O Christ, wash out this blood!" [The History of the Evangelical Churches of the Valleys of Piedmont: containing a most exact Geographical Description of the place, and a faithful Account of the Doctrine, Life, and Persecutions of the ancient Inhabitants, together with a most naked and punctual Relation of the late bloody Massacre, 1655. By Samuel Morland, Esq., His Highness' Commissioner Extraordinary for the Affairs of the said Valleys. London, 1658.]

We have repeatedly mentioned the Castelluzzo in our narrative of this people and their many martyrdoms. It is closely connected with the Massacre of 1655, and as such kindled the muse of Milton. It stands at the entrance of the Valleys, its feet swathed in feathery woods; above which is a mass of debris and fallen rocks, which countless tempests have gathered like a girdle round its middle. From amidst these the supreme column shoots up, pillar-like, and touches that white cloud which is floating past in mid-heaven. One can see a dark spot on the face of the cliff just below the crowning rocks of the summit. It would be taken for the shadow of a passing cloud upon the mountain, were it not that it is immovable. That is the mouth of a cave so roomy, it is said, as to be able to contain some hundreds. To this friendly chamber the Waldenses were wont to flee when the valley beneath was a perfect Pandemonium, glittering with steel, red with crime, and ringing with execrations and blasphemies. To this cave many of the Vaudois fled on occasion of the great massacre. But, alas! thither the persecutor tracked them, and dragging them forth rolled them down the awful precipice.

The law that indissolubly links great crimes with the spot where they were perpetrated, has written the Massacre of 1655 on this mountain, and given it in eternal keeping to its rock. There is not another such martyrs' monument in the whole world. While the Castelluzzo stands the memory of this great crime cannot die; through all the ages it will continue to cry, and that cry our sublimest poet has interpreted in his sublime sonnet:--

> "Avenge, O Lord, Thy slaughtered saints, whose bones
> Lie scattered on the Alpine mountains cold;
> Even them who kept Thy truth so pure of old,
> When all our fathers worshipt stocks and stones,
> Forget not: in Thy book record their groans
> Who were Thy sheep, and in their ancient fold
> Slain by the bloody Piedmontese, that roll'd
> Mother with infant down the rocks. Their moans
> The vales redoubled to the hills, and they
> To heaven. Their martyr'd blood and ashes sow
> O'er all the Italian fields, where still doth sway
> The triple tyrant; that from these may grow
> A hundredfold, who having learned Thy way,
> Early may fly the Babylonian woe."

CHAPTER 14
Exploits of Gianavello—Massacre and Pillage of Rora

The next tragic episode in the history of the Waldenses takes us to the Valley of Rora. The invasion and outrages of which this valley became the scene were contemporaneous with the horrors of the great massacre. In what we are now to relate, feats of heroism are blended with deeds of suffering, and we are called to admire the valor of the patriot, as well as the patience of the martyr.

The Valley of Rora lies on the left as one enters La Torre; it is separated from Lucerna by a barrier of mountains. Rora has two entrances: one by a side ravine, which branches off about two miles before reaching La Torre, and the other by crossing the Valley of Lucerna and climbing the mountains. This last is worthy of being briefly described. We start, let us suppose, from the town of La Torre; we skirt the Castelluzzo on the right, which high in air hangs its precipices, with their many tragic memories, above us. From this point we turn to the left, descend into the valley, traverse its bright meadows, here shaded by the vine which stretches its arms in classic freedom from tree to tree. We cross the torrent of the Pelice by a small bridge, and hold on our way till we reach the foot of the mountains of La Combe, that wall in the Valley of Rora. We begin to climb by a winding path. Pasturage and vineyard give place to chestnut forest; the chestnut in its turn yields to the pine; and, as we mount still higher, we find ourselves amid the naked ledges of the mountain, with their gushing rills, margined by moss or other Alpine herbage.

An ascent of two hours brings us to the summit of the pass. We have here a pedestal, some 4,000 feet in height, in the midst of a stupendous amphitheatre of

Alps, from which to view their glories. How profoundly deep the valley from which we have just climbed up! A thread of silver is now the Pelice; a patch of green a few inches square is now the meadow; the chestnut-tree is a mere dot, hardly visible; and yonder are La Torre and the white Villaro, so tiny that they look as if they could be packed into a child's toy-box.

But while all else has diminished, the mountains seem to have enlarged their bulk and increased their stature. High above us towers the summit of the Castelluzzo; still higher rise the rolling masses of the Vandalin, the lower slopes of which form a vast and magnificent hanging garden, utterly dwarfing those which were among the wonders of Babylon. And in the far distance the eye rests on a tumultuous sea of mountains, here rising in needles, there running off in long serrated ridges, and there standing up in massive peaks of naked granite, wearing the shining garments which winter weaves for the giants of the Alps.

We now descend into the Valley of Rora. It lies at our feet, a cup of verdure, some sixty miles in circumference, its sides and bottom variously clothed with corn-field and meadow, with vineyard and orchard, with the walnut, the cherry, and all fruit-bearing trees, from amid which numerous brown chalets peep out. The great mountains sweep round the valley like a wall, and among them, pre-eminent in glory as in stature, stands the monarch of the Cottian Alps-Monte Viso.

As among the Jews of old, so among the Waldenses, God raised up, from time to time, mighty men of valor to deliver his people. One of the most remarkable of these men was Gianavello, commonly known as Captain Joshua Gianavello, a native of this same Valley of Rora. He appears, from the accounts that have come down to us, to have possessed all the qualities of a great military leader. He was a man of daring courage, of resolute purpose, and of venturous enterprise. He had the faculty, so essential in a commander, of skilful combination. He was fertile in resource, and self-possessed in emergencies; he was quick to resolve, and prompt to execute. His devotion and energy were the means, under God, of mitigating somewhat the horrors of the Massacre of 1655, and his heroism ultimately rolled back the tide of that great calamity, and made it recoil upon its authors. It was the morning of the 24th of April, 1655, the day which saw the butchery commenced that we have described above. On that same day 500 soldiers were dispatched by the Marquis de Pianeza to the Valley of Rora, to massacre its unoffending and unsuspecting inhabitants. Ascending from the Valley of the Pelice, they had gained the summit of the pass, and were already descending on the town of Rora, stealthily and swiftly, as a herd of wolves might descend upon a sheep-fold, or as, says Leger, "a brood of vultures might descend upon a flock of harmless doves." Happily Gianavello, who had known for weeks before that a storm was gathering, though he knew not when or where it would burst, was on the outlook. He saw the troop, and guessed their errand. There was not a moment to be lost; a little longer, and not a man would be left alive in Rora to carry tidings of its fate to the next commune. But was Gianavello single-handed to attack an army of 500 men? He stole up-hill, under cover of the rocks and trees, and on his way he prevailed on six peasants, brave men like himself, to join him in repelling the invaders. The heroic little band marched on till they were near the troop, then hiding amid the bushes, they lay in ambush by the side of the path. The soldiers came on, little suspecting the trap into which they were marching. Gianavello and his men fired, and with so unerring an aim that seven of the troop fell dead. Then, reloading their pieces, and dexterously changing their ground, they fired again with a like effect. The attack was unexpected; the foe was invisible; the frightened imaginations of Pianeza's soldiers multiplied tenfold the number of their assailants. They began to retreat. But Gianavello and his men, bounding from cover to cover like so many chamois, hung upon their rear, and did deadly execution with their bullets. The invaders left 54 of their number dead behind them; and thus did these seven peasants chase from their Valley of Rora the 500 assassins who had come to murder its peaceful inhabitants [Leger, part ii., chap. 11, p. 186].

That same afternoon the people of Rora, who were ignorant of the fearful murders which were at that very moment proceeding in the valleys of their brethren, repaired to the Marquis de Pianeza to complain of the attack. The marquis affected ignorance of the whole affair. "Those who invaded your valley," said he, "were a set of banditti. You did right to repel them. Go back to your families and fear nothing; I pledge my word and honor that no evil shall happen to you."

These deceitful words did not impose upon Gianavello. He had a wholesome recollection of the maxim enacted by the Council of Constance, and so often put in practice in the Valleys, "No faith is to be kept with heretics." Pianeza, he knew, was the agent of the "Council of Extirpation." Hardly had the next morning broken when the hero-peasant was abroad, scanning with eagle-eye the mountain paths that led into his valley. It was not long till his suspicions were more than justified. Six hundred men-at-arms, chosen with special reference to this difficult enterprise, were seen ascending the mountain Cassuleto, to do what their comrades of the previous day had failed to accomplish. Gianavello had now mustered a little host of eighteen, of whom twelve were armed with muskets and swords, and six with only the sling. These he divided into three parties, each consisting of four musketeers and two slingers, and he posted them in a defile, through which he saw the invaders must pass. No sooner had the van of the enemy entered the gore than a shower of bullets and stones from invisible hands saluted them. Every bullet and stone did its work. The first discharge brought down an officer and twelve men. That volley was succeeded by others equally fatal. The cry was raised, "All is lost, save yourselves!" The flight was precipitate, for every bush and rock seemed to vomit forth deadly missiles. Thus a second ignominious retreat rid the Valley of Rora of these murderers.

The inhabitants carried their complaints a second time to Pianeza. "Concealing," as Leger says, "the ferocity of the tiger under the skin of the fox," he assured the deputies that the attack had been the result of a misunderstanding; that certain accusations had been lodged against them, the falsity of which had since been discovered, and now they might return to their homes, for they had nothing to fear. No sooner were they gone than Pianeza began vigorously to prepare for a third attack [Leger, part ii., pp. 186-7].

He organized a battalion of from 800 to 900 men. Next morning, this host made a rapid march on Rora, seized all the avenues leading into the valley, and chasing the inhabitants to the caves in Monte Friolante, set fire to their dwellings, having first plundered them. Captain Joshua Gianavello, at the head of his little troop, saw the enemy enter, but their numbers were so overwhelming that he waited a more favorable moment for attacking them. The soldiers were retiring, laden with their booty, and driving before them the cattle of the peasants. Gianavello knelt down before his hero-band, and giving thanks to God, who had twice by his hand saved his people, he prayed that the hearts and arms of his followers might be strengthened, to work yet another deliverance. He then attacked the foe. The spoilers turned and then fled up-hill, in the hope of escaping into the Valley of the Pelice, throwing away their booty in their flight. When they had gained the pass, and begun their descent, their flight became yet more disastrous; great stones, torn up and rolled after them, were mingled with the bullets, and did deadly execution upon them, while the precipices over which they fell in their haste consummated their destruction. The few who survived fled to Villaro [Leger, part ii., p. 187. Muston, pp. 146-7].

The Marquis de Pianeza, instead of seeing in these events the finger of God, was only the more inflamed with rage, and the more resolutely bent on the extirpation of every heretic from the Valley of Rora. He assembled all the royal troops then under his command, or which could be spared from the massacre in which they were occupied in the other valleys, in order to surround the little territory. This was now the fourth attack on the commune of Rora, but the invaders were destined once more to recoil before the shock of its heroic defenders. Some 8,000 men had been got under arms, and were ready to march against Rora, but the impatience of a certain Captain Mario, who had signalized himself in the massacre at Bobbio, and wished to appropriate the entire glory of the enterprise, would not permit him to await the movement of the main body. He marched two hours in advance, with three companies of regular troops, few of whom ever returned. Their ferocious leader, borne along by the rush of his panic-stricken soldiers, was precipitated over the edge of the rock into the stream, and badly bruised. He was drawn out and carried to Lucerna, where he died two days afterwards, in great torment of body, and yet greater torment of mind. Of the three companies which he led in this fatal expedition, one was composed of Irish, who had been banished by Cromwell, and who met in this distant land the death they had inflicted on others in their own, leaving their corpses to fatten those valleys which were to have been theirs had they succeeded in purging them of heresy and heretics [Leger, part ii., p. 188. Muston, pp. 148-9].

This series of strange events was now drawing to an end. The fury of Pianeza knew no bounds. This war of his, though waged only with herdsmen, had brought him nothing but disgrace, and the loss of his bravest soldiers. Victor Amadeus once observed that "the skin of every Vaudois cost him fifteen of his best Piedmontese soldiers." Pianeza had lost some hundreds of his best soldiers, and yet not one of the little troop of Gianavello, dead or alive, had he been able to get into his hands. Nevertheless, he resolved to continue the struggle, but with a much greater army. He assembled 10,000, and attacked Rora on three sides at once. While Gianavello was bravely combating with the first troop of 3,000, on the summit of the pass that gives entrance from the Valley of the Pelice, a second of 6,000 had entered by the ravine at the foot of the valley; and a third of 1,000 had crossed the mountains that divide Bagnolo from Rora. But, alas! who shall describe the horrors that followed the entrance of these assassins? Blood, burning, and rapine in an instant overwhelmed the little community. No distinction was made of age or sex. None had pity for their tender years; none had reverence for their grey hairs. Happy they who were slain at once, and thus escaped horrible indignities and tortures. The few spared from the sword were carried away as captives, and among these were the wife and the three daughters of Gianavello [Leger, part ii., p. 189. Monastier, p. 277].

There was now nothing more in the Valley of Rora for which the patriot-hero could do battle. The light of his hearth was quenched, his village was a heap of smoking ruins, his fathers and brethren had fallen by the sword; but rising superior to these accumulated calamities, he marched his little troop over the mountains, to await on the frontier of his country whatever opportunities Providence might yet open to him of wielding his sword in defense of the ancient liberties and the glorious faith of his people.

It was at this time that Pianeza, intending to deal the finishing blow that should crush the hero of Rora, wrote to Gianavello as follows:--"I exhort you for the last time to renounce your heresy. This is the only hope of your obtaining the pardon of your prince, and of saving the life of your wife and daughters, now my prisoners, and whom, if you continue obstinate, I will burn alive. As for yourself, my soldiers shall no longer pursue you, but I will set such a price upon your head, as that, were you Beelzebub himself, you shall infallibly be taken; and be assured that, if you fall alive into my hands, there are no torments with which I will not punish your rebellion." To these ferocious threats Gianavello magnanimously and promptly replied: "There are no torments so terrible, no death so barbarous, that I would not choose rather than deny my Savior. Your threats cannot cause me to renounce my faith; they but fortify me in it. Should the Marquis de Pianeza cause my wife and daughters to pass through the fire, it can but consume their mortal bodies; their souls I commend to God, trusting that he will have mercy on them, and on mine, should it please him that I fall into the marquis's hands" [Leger, part ii., p. 189]. We do not know whether Pianeza was capable of seeing that this was the most mortifying defeat he had yet sustained at the hands of the peasant-hero of Rora; and that he might as well war against the Alps themselves as against a cause that could infuse a spirit like this into its champions. Gianavello's reply, observes Leger, "certified him as a chosen instrument in the hands of God for the recovery of his country seemingly lost."

Gianavello had saved from the wreck of his family his infant son, and his first care was to seek a place of safety for him. Laying him on his shoulders, he passed the frozen Alps which separate the Valley of Lucerna from France, and entrusted the child to the care of a relative resident at Queyras, in the Valleys of the French Protestants. With the child he carried thither the tidings of the awful massacre of his people. Indignation was roused. Not a few were willing to join his standard, brave spirits like himself; and, with his little band greatly recruited, he repassed the Alps in a few weeks, to begin his second and more successful campaign. On his arrival in the Valleys he was joined by Giaheri, under whom a troop had been assembling to avenge the massacre of their brethren.

In Giaheri, Captain Gianavello had found a companion worthy of himself, and worthy of the cause for which he was now in arms. Of this heroic man Leger has recorded that, "though he possessed the courage of a lion, he was as humble as a lamb, always giving to God the glory of his victories; well versed in Scripture, and understanding controversy, and of great natural talent." The massacre had reduced the Vaudois race to all but utter extermination, and 50 men were all that the two leaders could collect around their standard. The army opposed to them, and at this time in their Valleys, was from 15,000 to 20,000 strong, consisting of trained and picked soldiers. Nothing but an impulse from the God of battles could have moved these two men, with such a handful, to take the field against such odds. To the eye of a common hero all would have seemed lost; but the courage of these two

Christian warriors was based on faith. They believed that God would not permit his cause to perish, or the lamp of the Valleys to be extinguished; and, few though they were, they knew that God was able by their humble instrumentality to save their country and Church. In this faith they unsheathed the sword; and so valiantly did they wield it, that soon that sword became the terror of the Piedmontese armies. The ancient promise was fulfilled, "The people that do know their God shall be strong and do exploits."

We cannot go into details. Prodigies of valor were performed by this little host. "I had always considered the Vaudois to be men," said Descombies, who had joined them, "but I found them lions." Nothing could withstand the fury of their attack. Post after post and village after village were wrested from the Piedmontese troops. Soon the enemy was driven from the upper valleys. The war now passed down into the plain of Piedmont, and there it was waged with the same heroism and the same success. They besieged and took several towns, they fought not a few pitched battles; and in those actions they were nearly always victorious, though opposed by more than ten times their number. Their success could hardly be credited had it not been recorded by historians whose veracity is above suspicion, and the accuracy of whose statements was attested by eye-witnesses. Not unfrequently did it happen at the close of a day's fighting that 1,400 Piedmontese dead covered the field of battle, while not more than six or seven of the Waldenses had fallen. Such success might well be termed miraculous; and not only did it appear so to the Vaudois themselves, but even to their foes, who could not refrain from expressing their conviction "that surely God was on the side of the Barbets."

While the Vaudois were thus heroically maintaining their cause by arms, and rolling back the chastisement of war on those from whom its miseries had come, tidings of their wrongs were traveling to all the Protestant States of Europe. Wherever these tidings came a felling of horror was evoked, and the cruelty of the Government of Savoy was universally and loudly execrated. All confessed that such a tale of woe they had never before heard. But the Protestant States did not content themselves with simply condemning these deeds; they judged it to be their clear duty to move in behalf of this poor and greatly oppressed people; and foremost among those who did themselves lasting honor by interposing in behalf of a people "drawn unto death and ready to perish," was, as has already been said, England, then under the protectorate of Cromwell. In the previous chapter mention was made of the Latin letter, the composition of Milton, which the Protector addressed to the Duke of Savoy. In addition, Cromwell wrote to Louis XIV of France, soliciting his mediation with the duke in behalf of the Vaudois. The letter is interesting as containing the truly catholic and noble sentiments of England, to which the pen of her great poet gave fitting expression:--

> "Most Serene and Potent King, ... After a most barbarous slaughter of persons of both sexes, and of all ages, a treaty of peace was concluded, or rather secret acts of hostility were committed the more securely under the name of a pacification. The conditions of the treaty were determined in your town of Pinerolo: hard conditions enough, but such as these poor people would gladly have agreed to, after the horrible outrages to which they had been exposed, provided that they had been faithfully observed. But they were not observed; the meaning of the treaty is evaded and violated, by putting a false interpretation upon some of the articles, and by straining others. Many of the complainants have been deprived of their patrimonies, and many have been forbidden the exercise of their religion. New payments have been exacted, and a new fort has been built to keep them in check, from whence a disorderly soldiery makes frequent sallies, and plunders or murders all it meets. In addition to these things, fresh levies of troops are clandestinely preparing to march against them; and those among them who profess the Roman Catholic religion have been advised to retire in time; so that everything threatens the speedy destruction of such as escaped the former massacre. I do therefore beseech and conjure your Majesty not to suffer such enormities, and not to permit (I will not say any prince, for surely such barbarity never could enter into the heart of a prince, much less of one of the duke's tender age, or into the mind of his mother) those accursed murderers to indulge in such savage ferocity, who, while they profess to be the servants and followers of Christ, who came into the world to save sinners, do blaspheme his name, and transgress his mild precepts, by the slaughter of innocent men. Oh, that your Majesty, who has the power, and who ought to be inclined to use it, may deliver so many supplicants from the hands of murderers, who are already drunk with blood, and thirst for it again, and who take pleasure in throwing the odium of their cruelty upon princes! I implore your Majesty not to suffer the borders of your kingdom to be polluted by such monstrous wickedness. Remember that this very race of people threw itself upon the protection of your grandfather, King Henry IV, who was most friendly disposed towards the Protestants, when the Duke of Lesdiguieres passed victoriously through their country; as affording the most commodious passage into Italy at the time he pursued the Duke of Savoy in his retreat across the Alps. The act or instrument of that submission is still extant among the public records of your kingdom, in which it is provided that the Vaudois shall not be transferred to any other

government, but upon the same condition that they were received under the protection of your invincible grandfather. As supplicants of his grandson, they now implore the fulfillment of this compact.
"Given at our Court at Westminster, this 26th of May, 1658."

The French King undertook the mediation, as requested by the Protestant princes, but hurried it to a conclusion before the ambassadors from the Protestant States had arrived. The delegates from the Protestant cantons of Switzerland were present, but they were permitted to act the part of onlookers simply. The Grand Monarch took the whole affair upon himself, and on the 18th of August, 1655, a treaty of peace was concluded of a very disadvantageous kind. The Waldenses were stripped of their ancient possessions on the right bank of the Pelice, lying toward the plain of Piedmont. Within the new boundary they were guaranteed liberty of worship; an amnesty was granted for all offences committed during the war; captives were to be restored when claimed; and they were to be exempt from all imposts for five years, on the ground that they were so impoverished as not to be able to pay anything.

When the treaty was published it was found to contain two clauses that astonished the Protestant world. In the preamble the Vaudois were styled rebels, whom it had pleased their prince graciously to receive back into favor; and in the body of the deed was an article, which no one recollected to have heard mentioned during the negotiations, empowering the French to construct a fort above La Torre. This looked like a preparation for renewing the war.

By this treaty the Protestant States were outwitted; their ambassadors were duped; and the poor Vaudois were left as much as ever in the power of the Duke of Savoy and of the Council for the Propagation of the Faith and the Extirpation of Heretics.

CHAPTER 15
The Exile

After the great Massacre of 1655, the Church of the Valleys had rest from persecution for thirty years. This period, however, can be styled one of rest only when contrasted with the frightful storms which had convulsed the era that immediately preceded it. The enemies of the Vaudois still found innumerable ways in which to annoy and harass them. Ceaseless intrigues were continually breeding new alarms, and the Vaudois had often to till their fields and prune their vines with their muskets slung across their shoulders. Many of their chief men were sent into exile. Captain Gianavello and Pastor Leger, whose services to their people were too great ever to be forgiven, had sentence of death passed on them. Leger "was to be strangled; then his body was to be hung by one foot on a gibbet for four-and-twenty hours; and, lastly, his head was to be cut off and publicly exposed at San Giovanni. His name was to be inserted in the list of noted outlaws; his houses were to be burned" [Leger, part ii., p. 275]. Gianavello retired to Geneva, where he continued to watch with unabated interest the fortunes of his people. Leger became pastor of a congregation at Leyden, where he crowned a life full of labor and suffering for the Gospel, by a work which has laid all Christendom under obligations to him; we refer to his History of the Churches of the Vaudois–a noble monument of his Church's martyr-heroism and his own Christian patriotism.

Hardly had Leger unrolled to the world's gaze the record of the last awful tempest which had smitten the Valleys, when the clouds returned, and were seen rolling up in dark, thunderous masses against this devoted land. Former storms had assailed them from the south, having collected in the Vatican; the tempest now approaching had its first rise on the north of the Alps. It was the year 1685; Louis XIV was nearing the grave, and with the great Audit in view he inquired of his confessor by what good deed as a king he might atone for his many sins as a man. The answer was ready. He was told that he must extirpate Protestantism in France.

The Grand Monarch, as the age styled him, bowed obsequiously before the shaven crown of priest, while Europe was trembling before his armies. Louis XIV did as he was commanded; he revoked the Edict of Nantes. This gigantic crime inflicted no less misery on the Protestants than it brought countless woes on the throne and nation of France. But it is the nation of the Vaudois, and the persecution which the counsel of Pere la Chaise brought upon them, with which we have here to do. Wishing for companionship in the sanguinary work of purging France from Protestantism, Louis XIV sent an ambassador to the Duke of Savoy, with a request that he would deal with the Waldenses as he was now dealing with the Huguenots. The young and naturally humane Victor Amadeus was at the moment on more than usually friendly terms with his subjects of the Valleys. They had served bravely under his standard in his late war with the Genoese, and he had but recently written them a letter of thanks. How could he unsheathe his sword against the men whose devotion and valor had so largely contributed to his victory? Victor Amadeus deigned no reply to the French ambassador. The request was repeated; it received an evasive answer; it was urged a third time, accompanied by a hint from the potent Louis that if it was not convenient for the duke to purge his dominions, the King of France would do it for him with an army of 14,000 men, and would keep the Valleys for his pains. This was enough. A treaty was immediately concluded between the duke and the French King, in which the latter promised an armed force to enable the former to reduce the Vaudois to the Roman obedience, or to exterminate them [Monastier, p. 311]. On the 31st of January, 1686, the following edict was promulgated in the Valleys:

> 1. the Vaudois shall henceforth and for ever cease and discontinue all the exercises of their religion.
> 2. They are forbidden to have religious meetings, under pain of death, and penalty of confiscation of all their goods.
> 3. All their ancient privileges are abolished.
> 4. All the churches, prayer-houses, and other edifices consecrated to their worship shall be razed to the ground.

5. All the pastors and schoolmasters of the Valleys are required either to embrace Romanism or to quit the country within fifteen days, under pain of death and confiscation of goods.

6. All the children born, or to be born, of Protestant parents shall be compulsorily trained up as Roman Catholics. Every such child yet unborn shall, within a week after its birth, be brought to the cure of its parish, and admitted of the Roman Catholic Church, under pain, on the part of the mother, of being publicly whipped with rods, and on the part of the father of laboring five years in the galleys.

7. The Vaudois pastors shall abjure the doctrine they have hitherto publicly preached; shall receive a salary, greater by one-third than that which they previously enjoyed; and one-half thereof shall go in reversion to their widows.

8. All Protestant foreigners settled in Piedmont are ordered either to become Roman Catholics, or to quit the country within fifteen days.

9. By a special act of his great and paternal clemency, the sovereign will permit persons to sell, in this interval, the property they may have acquired in Piedmont, provided the sale be made to Roman Catholic purchasers."

This monstrous edict seemed to sound the knell of the Vaudois as a Protestant people. Their oldest traditions did not contain a decree so cruel and unrighteous, nor one that menaced them with so complete and summary a destruction as that which now seemed to impend over them. What was to be done? Their first step was to send delegates to Turin, respectfully to remind the duke that the Vaudois had inhabited the Valleys from the earliest times; that they had led forth their herds upon their mountains before the House of Savoy had ascended the throne of Piedmont; that treaties and oaths, renewed from reign to reign, had solemnly secured them in the freedom of their worship and other liberties; and that the honor of princes and the stability of States lay in the faithful observance of such covenants; and they prayed him to consider what reproach the throne and kingdom of Piedmont would incur if he should become the executioner of those of whom he was the natural protector. The Protestant cantons of Switzerland joined their mediations to the intercession of the Waldenses. And when the almost incredible edict came to be known in Germany and Holland, these countries threw their shield over the Valleys, by interceding with the duke that he would not inflict so great a wrong as to cast out from a land which was theirs by irrevocable charters, a people whose only crime was that they worshipped as their fathers had worshipped, before they passed under the scepter of the duke. All these powerful parties pleaded in vain. Ancient charters, solemn treaties, and oaths, made in the face of Europe, the long-tried loyalty and the many services of the Vaudois to the House of Savoy, could not stay the uplifted arm of the duke, or prevent the execution of the monstrously criminal decree. In a little while the armies of France and Savoy arrived before the Valleys.

At no previous period of their history, perhaps, had the Waldenses been so entirely devoid of human aid as now. Gianavello, whose stout heart and brave arm had stood them in such stead formerly, was in exile. Cromwell, whose potent voice had stayed the fury of the great massacre, was in his grave. An avowed Papist filled the throne of Great Britain. It was going ill at this hour with Protestantism everywhere. The Covenanters of Scotland were hiding on the moors, or dying in the Grass-market of Edinburgh. France, Piedmont, and Italy were closing in around the Valleys; every path guarded, all their succors cut off, an overwhelming force waited the signal to massacre them. So desperate did their situation appear to the Swiss envoys, that they counseled them to "transport elsewhere the torch of the Gospel, and not keep it here to be extinguished in blood."

The proposal to abandon their ancient inheritance, coming from such a quarter, startled the Waldenses. It produced, at first, a division of opinion in the Valleys, but ultimately they united in rejecting it. They remembered the exploits their fathers had done, and the wonders God had wrought in the mountain passes of Rora, in the defiles of Angrogna, and in the field of the Pra del Tor, and their faith reviving, they resolved, in a reliance on the same Almighty Arm which had been stretched out in their behalf in former days, to defend their hearths and altars. They repaired the old defenses, and made ready for resistance. On the 17th of April, being Good Friday, they renewed their covenant, and on Easter Sunday their pastors dispensed to them the Communion. This was the last time the sons of the Valleys partook of the Lord's Supper before their great dispersion.

Victor Amadeus II had pitched his camp on the plain of San Gegonzo before the Vaudois Alps. His army consisted of five regiments of horse and foot. He was here joined by the French auxiliaries who had crossed the Alps, consisting of some dozen battalions, the united force amounting to between 15,000 and 20,000 men. The signal was to be given on Easter Monday, at break of day, by three cannon-shots, fired from the hill of Bricherasio. On the appointed morning, the Valleys of Lucerna and San Martino, forming the two extreme opposite points of the territory, were attacked, the first by the Piedmontese host, and the last by the French, under the command of General Catinat, a distinguished soldier. In San Martino the fighting lasted ten hours, and ended in a complete repulse of the French, who retired at night with a loss of more than 500 killed and wounded, while the Vaudois had lost only two [Monastier, p. 317. Muston, p. 199]. On the following day the French, burning with rage at their defeat, poured a more numerous army into San Martino, which swept along the valley, burning, plundering, and massacring, and having crossed the mountains descended into Pramol, continuing the same indiscriminate and exterminating vengeance. To the rage of the sword were added other barbarities and outrages too shocking to be narrated [Muston, p. 200].

The issue by arms being deemed uncertain, despite the vast disparity of strength, treachery, on a great scale, was now had recourse to. Wherever, throughout the Valleys, the Vaudois were found strongly posted, and ready for battle, they were told that their brethren in the neighboring communes had submitted, and that it was vain for them, isolated and alone as they now were, to continue their resistance. When they sent deputies to head-quarters to inquire-and passes were freely supplied to them for that purpose-they were assured that the submission had been universal, and that none save themselves were now in arms. They were assured, moreover, that should they follow the example of the rest of their nation, all their ancient liberties would be held intact [Muston, p. 202]. This base artifice was successfully practiced at each of the Vaudois posts in succession, till at length the Valleys had all capitulated. We cannot blame the Waldenses, who were the victims of an act so dishonorable and vile as hardly to be credible; but the mistake, alas! was a fatal one, and had to be expiated afterwards by the endurance of woes a hundred times more dreadful than any they would have encountered in the rudest campaign. The instant consequence of the submission was a massacre which extended to all their Valleys, and which was similar in its horrors to the great butchery of 1655. In that massacre upwards of 3,000 perished. The remainder of the nation, amounting, according to Arnaud, to between 12,000 and 15,000 souls, were consigned to the various gaols and fortresses of Piedmont [Monastier, p. 320].

We now behold these famous Valleys, for the first time in their history, empty. The ancient lamp burns no longer. The school of the prophets in the Pra del Tor is razed. No smoke is seen rising from cottage, and no psalm is heard ascending from dwelling or sanctuary. No herdsman leads forth his kine on the mountains, and no troop of worshippers, obedient to the summons of the Sabbath-bell, climbs the mountain paths. The vine flings wide her arms, but no skilful hand is nigh to train her boughs and prune her luxuriance. The chestnut tree rains its fruits, but there is no troop of merry children to gather them, and they lie rotting on the ground. The terraces of the hills, that were wont to overflow with flowers and fruitage, and which presented to the eye a series of hanging gardens, now torn and breached, shoot in a mass of ruinous rubbish down the slope. Nothing is seen but dismantled forts, and the blacked ruins of churches and hamlets. A dreary silence overspreads the land, and the beasts of the field strangely multiply. A few herdsmen, hidden here and there in forests and holes of the rocks, are now the only inhabitants. monte Viso, from out the silent vault, looks down with astonishment at the absence of that ancient race over whom, from immemorial time, he had been wont to dart his kindling glories at dawn, and let fall at eve in purple shadows the ample folds of his friendly mantle.

We know not if ever before an entire nation were in prison at once. Yet now it was so. All of the Waldensian race that remained from the sword of their executioners were immured in the dungeons of Piedmont! The pastor and his flock, the father and his family, the patriarch and the stripling had passed in, in one great procession, and exchanged their grand rock-walled Valleys, their tree-embowered homes, and their sunlit peaks, for the filth, the choking air, and the Tartarean walls of an Italian gaol. And how were they treated in prison? As the African slave was treated on the "middle passage." They had a sufficiency of neither food nor clothing. The bread dealt out to them was fetid. They had putrid water to drink. They were exposed to the sun by day and to the cold at night. They were compelled to sleep on the bare pavement, or on straw so full of vermin that the stone floor was preferable. Disease broke out in these horrible abodes, and the mortality was fearful. "When they entered these dungeons," says Henri Arnaud, "they counted 14,000 healthy mountaineers; but when, at the intercession of the Swiss deputies, their prisons were opened, 3,000 skeletons only crawled out." These few words portray a tragedy so awful that the imagination recoils from the contemplation of it.

However, at length the persecutor looses their chains, and opening their prison doors he sends forth these captives-the woe-worn remnant of a gallant people. But to what are they sent forth? To people again their ancient Valleys? To rekindle the fire on their ancestral hearths? To rebuild "the holy and beautiful house" in which their fathers had praised God? Ah, no! They are thrust out of prison only to be sent into exile-to Vaudois a living death.

The barbarity of 1655 was repeated. It was in December (1686) that the decree of liberation was issued in favor of these 3,000 men who had escaped the sword, and now survived the not less deadly epidemic of the prison. At that season, as every one knows, the snow and ice are piled to a fearful depth on the Alps; and daily tempests threaten with death the too adventurous traveler who would cross their summits. It was at this season that these poor captives, emaciated with sickness, weakened by hunger, and shivering from insufficient clothing, were commanded to rise up and cross the snowy hills. They began their journey on the afternoon of that very day on which the order arrived; for their enemies would permit no delay. One hundred and fifty of them died on their first march. At night they halted at the foot of the Mont Cenis. Next morning, when they surveyed the Alps they saw evident signs of a gathering tempest, and they besought the officer in charge to permit them, for the sake of their sick and aged, to remain where they were till the storm had spent its rage. With heart harder than the rocks they were to traverse, the officer ordered them to resume their journey. That troop of emaciated beings began the ascent, and were soon struggling with the blinding drifts and fearful whirlwinds of the mountain. Eighty-six of their number, succumbing to the tempest, dropped by the way. Where they lay down, there they died. No relative or friend was permitted to remain behind to watch their last moments or tender them needed succor. That ever-thinning procession moved on and on over the white hills, leaving it to the falling snow to give burial to their stricken companions. When spring opened the passes of the Alps, alas! what ghastly memorials met the eye of the horror-stricken traveler. Strewed along the track were the now unshrouded corpses of these poor exiles, the dead child lying fast locked in the arms of the dead mother.

But why should we prolong this harrowing tale? The first company of these miserable exiles arrived at Geneva on Christmas Day, 1686, having spent about three weeks on the journey. They were followed by small parties, who crossed the Alps one after the other, being let out of prison at different times. It was not till the end of February, 1687, that the last band of these emigrants reached the hospitable gates of Geneva. But in what a plight! way-worn, sick, emaciated, and faint through hunger. Of some the tongue was swollen in their mouth, and they were unable to speak; of others the arms were bitten with the frost, so that they could not stretch them out to accept the charity offered to them; and some there were who dropped down and expired on the very threshold of the city, "finding," as one has said, "the end of their life at the beginning of their liberty." Most hospitable was the reception given them by the city of Calvin. A deputation of the principal citizens of Geneva, headed by the patriarch Gianavello, who still lived, went out to meet them on the frontier, and taking them to their homes, vied with each other which should show them the greatest kindness. Generous city! If he who shall give a cup of cold water to a disciple shall in nowise lose his reward, how much more shalt thou be requited for this thy kindness to the suffering and sorrowing exiles of the Savior!

CHAPTER 16
Return to the Valleys

Now we open the bright page of the Vaudois history. We have seen nearly 3,000 Waldensian exiles enter the gates of Geneva, the feeble remnant of a population of from 14,000 to 16,000. One city could not contain them all, and arrangements were made for distributing the expatriated Vaudois among the Reformed cantons. The revocation of the Edict of Nantes had a little before thrown thousands of French Protestants upon the hospitality of the Swiss; and now the arrival of the Waldensian refugees brought with it yet heavier demands on the public and private charity of the cantons; but the response of Protestant Helvetia was equally cordial in the case of the last comers as in that of the first, and perhaps even more so, seeing their destitution was greater. Nor were the Vaudois ungrateful. "Next to God, whose tender mercies have preserved us from being entirely consumed," said they to their kind benefactors, "we are indebted to you alone for life and liberty."

Several of the German princes opened their States to these exiles; but the influence of their great enemy, Louis XIV, was then too powerful in these parts to permit of their residence being altogether an agreeable one. Constantly watched by his emissaries, and their patrons tampered with, they were moved about from place to place. The question of their permanent settlement in the future was beginning to be anxiously discussed. The project of carrying them across the sea in the ships of Holland, and planting them at the Cape, was even talked of. The idea of being separated for ever from their native land, dearer in exile than when they dwelt in it, gave them intolerable anguish. Was it not possible to reassemble their scattered colonies, and marching back to their Valleys, rekindle their ancient lamp in them? This was the question which, after three years of exile, the Vaudois began to put to themselves. As they wandered by the banks of the Rhine, or traversed the German plains, they feasted their imaginations on their far-off homes. The chestnuts shading their former abodes, the vine bending gracefully over their portal, and the meadow in front, which the crystal torrent kept perpetually bright, and whose murmur sweetly blended with the evening psalm, all rose before their eyes. They never knelt to pray but it was with their faces turned toward their grand mountains, where slept their martyred fathers. Attempts had been made by the Duke of Savoy to people their territory by settling in it a mongrel race, partly Irish and partly Piedmontese; but the land knew not the strangers, and refused to yield its strength to them. The Vaudois had sent spies to examine its condition [Monastier, p. 336]; its fields lay untilled, its vines unpruned, nor had its ruins been raised up; it was almost as desolate as on the day when its sons had been driven out of it. It seemed to them that the land was waiting their return.

At length the yearning of their heart could no longer be repressed. The march back to their Valleys is one of the most wonderful exploits ever performed by any people. It is famous in history by the name of "La Rentree Glorieuse." The parallel event which will recur to the mind of the scholar is, of course, the retreat of "the ten thousand Greeks." The patriotism and bravery of both will be admitted, but a candid comparison will, we think, incline one to assign the palm of heroism to the return of "the eight hundred."

The day fixed on for beginning their expedition was the 10th of June, 1688. Quitting their various cantonments in Switzerland, and traveling by by-roads, they traversed the country by night, and assembled at Bex, a small town in the southern extremity of the territory of Bern. Their secret march was soon known to the senates of Zurich, Bern, and Geneva; and, foreseeing that the departure of the exiles would compromise them with the Popish powers, their Excellencies took measures to prevent it. A bark laden with arms for their use was seized on the Lake of Geneva. The inhabitants of the Vallais, in concert with the Savoyards, at the first alarm seized the Bridge of St. Maurice, the key of the Rhone Valley, and stopped the expedition. Thus were they, for the time, compelled to abandon their project.

To extinguish all hopes of their return to the Valleys, they were anew distributed over Germany. But scarcely had this second dispersion been effected, when war broke out; the French troops overran the Palatinate, and the Vaudois settled there, dreading, not without reason, the soldiers of Louis XIV, retired before them, and retook the road to Switzerland. The Protestant cantons, pitying these poor exiles, tossed from country to country by political storms, settled them once more in their former allotments. Meanwhile, the scenes were shifting rapidly around the expatriated Vaudois, and with eyes uplifted they awaited the issue. They saw their protector, William of Orange, mount the throne of England. They saw their powerful enemy Louis XIV attacked at once by the emperor, and humiliated by the Dutch. They saw their own Prince Victor Amadeus withdraw his soldiers from Savoy, seeing that he needed them to defend Piedmont. It seemed to them that an invisible Hand was opening their path back to their own land. Encouraged by these tokens, they began to arrange a second time for their departure.

The place of appointed rendezvous was a wood on the northern shore of Lake Leman, near the town of Noyon. For days before they continued to converge, in scattered bands, and by stealthy marches, on the selected point. On the decisive evening, the 16th of August, 1689, a general muster took place under cover of the friendly wood of Prangins. Having by solemn prayer commended their enterprise to God, they embarked on the lake, and crossed by star-light. Their means of transport would have been deficient but for a circumstance which threatened at first to obstruct their expedition, but which, in the issue, greatly facilitated it. Curiosity had drawn numbers to this part of the lake, and the boats that brought hither the sight-seers furnished more amply the means of escape to the Vaudois.

At this crisis, as on so many previous ones, a distinguished man arose to lead them. Henri Arnaud, who was at the head of the 800 fighting men who now set out for their native possessions, had at first discharged the office of pastor, but the troubles of his nation compelling him to leave the Valleys, he had served in the armies of the Prince of Orange. Of decided piety, ardent patriotism, and of great decision and courage, he presented a beautiful instance of the union of the pastoral and the military character. It is hard to say whether his soldiers listened more reverentially to the exhortations he at times delivered to them from the pulpit, or to the orders he gave them on the field of battle.

Arriving on the southern shore of the lake, these 800 Vaudois bent their knees in prayer, and then began their march through a country covered with foes. Before them rose the great snow-clad mountains over which they were to fight their way. Arnaud arranged his little host into three companies–an advanced-guard, a centre, and a rear-guard. Seizing some of the chief men as hostages, they traversed the Valley of the Arve to Sallenches, and emerged from its dangerous passes just as the men of the latter place had completed their preparations for resisting them. Occasional skirmishes awaited them, but mostly their march was unopposed, for the terror of God had fallen upon the inhabitants of Savoy. Holding on their way they climbed the Haut Luce Alp, and next that of Bon Homme, the neighboring Alp to Mont Blanc, sinking sometimes to their middle in snow. Steep precipices and treacherous glaciers subjected them to both toil and danger. [The Haut Luce Alp was so named by the author of the Rentree, from the village at its foot, but which without doubt, says Monastier (p. 349), "is either the Col Joli (7,240 feet high) or the Col de la Fenetre, or Portetta, as it was named to Mr. Brockedon, who has visited these countries, and followed the same road as the Vaudois."] They were wet through with the rain, which at times fell in torrents. Their provisions were growing scanty, but their supply was recruited by the shepherds of the mountains, who brought them bread and cheese, while their huts served them at night. They renewed their hostages at every stage; sometimes they "caged"-to use their own phrase-a Capuchin monk, and at other times an influential landlord, but all were treated with uniform kindness.

Having crossed the Bon Homme, which divides the basin of the Arve from that of the Isere, they descended, on Wednesday, the fifth day of their march, into the valley of the latter stream. They had looked forward to this stage of their journey with great misgivings, for the numerous population of the Val Isere was known to be well armed, and decidedly hostile, and might be expected to oppose their march, but the enemy was "still as a stone" till the people had passed over. They next traversed Mont Iseran, and the yet more formidable Mont Cenis, and finally descended into the Valley of the Dora. It was here, on Saturday, the 24th of August, that they encountered for the first time a considerable body of regular troops.

As they traversed the valley they were met by a peasant, of whom they inquired whether they could have provisions by paying for them. "Come on this way," said the man, in a tone that had a slight touch of triumph in it, "you will find all that you want; they are preparing an excellent supper for you" [Monastier, p. 352]. They were led into the defile of Salabertrand, where the Col d'Albin closes in upon the stream of the Dora, and before they were aware they found themselves in presence of the French army, whose camp-fires-for night had fallen-illumined far and wide the opposite slope. Retreat was impossible. The French were 2,500 strong, flanked by the garrison of Exiles, and supported by a miscellaneous crowd of armed followers.

Under favor of the darkness, they advanced to the bridge which crossed the Dora, on the opposite bank of which the French were encamped. To the challenge, "Who goes there?" the Vaudois answered "Friends." The instant reply shouted out was "Kill, kill!" followed by a tremendous fire, which was kept up for a quarter of an hour. It did no harm, however, for Arnaud had bidden his soldiers lie flat on their faces, and permit the deadly shower to pass over them. But now a division of the French appeared in their rear, thus placing them between two fires. Some one in the Vaudois army, seeing that all must be risked, shouted out, "Courage! the bridge is won!" At those words the Vaudois started to their feet, rushed across the bridge sword in hand, and clearing it, they threw themselves with the impetuosity of a whirlwind upon the enemy's entrenchments. Confounded by the suddenness of the attack, the French could only use the butt-ends of their muskets to parry the blows. The fighting lasted two hours, and ended in the total rout of the French. Their leader, the Marquis de Larrey, after a fruitless attempt to rally his soldiers, fled wounded to Briancon exclaiming, "Is it possible that I have lost the battle and my honor?"

Soon thereafter the moon rose and showed the field of battle to the victors. On it, stretched out in death, lay 600 French soldiers, besides officers; and strewn promiscuously with the fallen, all over the field, were arms, military stores, and provisions. Thus had been suddenly opened an armory of magazines to men who stood much in need both of weapons and of food. Having amply replenished themselves, they collected what they could not carry away into a heap, and set fire to it. The loud and multifarious noises formed by the explosions of the gunpowder, the sounding of the trumpets, and the shouting of the captains, who, throwing their caps in the air, exclaimed, "Thanks be to the Lord of hosts, who hath given us the victory," echoed like the thunder of heaven, and reverberating from hill to hill, formed a most extraordinary and exciting scene, such as was seldom witnessed amid these usually quiet mountains. This great victory cost the Waldenses only fifteen killed and twelve wounded.

Their fatigue was great, but they feared to halt on the battle-field, and so, rousing those who had already sunk into sleep, they commenced climbing the lofty Mont Sci. The day was breaking as they gained the summit. It was Sunday, and Henri Arnaud, halting till all should assemble, pointed out to them, just as they were becoming visible in the morning light, the mountain-tops of their own land. Welcome sight to their longing eyes! Bathed in the radiance of the rising sun, it seemed to them, as one snowy peak began to burn after another, that the mountains were kindling into joy at the return of their long-absent sons. This army of soldiers resolved itself into a congregation of worshippers, and the summit of Mont Sci became their church. Kneeling on the mountain-top, the battle-field below them, and the solemn and sacred peaks of the Col du Pis, the Col la Vechera, and the glorious pyramid of Monte Viso looking down upon them in reverent silence, they humbled themselves before the Eternal, confessing their sins, and giving thanks for their many deliverances. Seldom has worship more sincere or more rapt been offered than that which this day ascended from this congregation of warrior-worshippers gathered under the dome-like vault that rose over them.

Refreshed by the devotions of the Sunday, and exhilarated by the victory of the day before, the heroic band now rushed down to take possession of their inheritance, from which the single Valley of Clusone only parted them. It was three years and a half since they had crossed the Alps, a crowd of exiles, worn to skeletons by sickness and confinement, and now they were returning, a marshaled host, victorious over the army of France, and ready to encounter that of Piedmont. They traversed the Clusone, a plain of about two miles in width, watered by the broad, clear, blue-tinted Garmagnasca, and bounded by hills, which offer to the eye a succession of terraces, clothed with the richest vines, mingled with the chestnut and the apple-tree. They entered the narrow defile of Pis, where a detachment of

Piedmontese soldiers had been posted to guard the pass, but who took flight at the approach of the Vaudois, thus opening to them the gate of one of the grandest of their Valleys, San Martino. On the twelfth day after setting out from the shores of Lake Leman they crossed the frontier, and stood once more within the limits of their inheritance. When they mustered at Balsiglia, the first Vaudois village which they entered, in the western extremity of San Martino, they found that fatigue, desertion, and battle had reduced their numbers from 800 to 700.

The first Sunday after their return was passed at the village of Prali. Of all their sanctuaries, the church of Prali alone remained standing; of the others only the ruins were to be seen. They resolved to commence this day their ancient and scriptural worship. Purging the church of its Popish ornaments, one half of the little army, laying down their arms at the door, entered the edifice, while the other half stood without, the church being too small to contain them all. Henri Arnaud, the soldier-pastor, mounting a table which was placed in the porch, preached to them. They began their worship by chanting the 74th Psalm-"O God, why hast thou cast us off for ever? Why doth thine anger smoke against the sheep of thy pasture?" The preacher then took as his text the 129th Psalm-"Many a time have they afflicted me from my youth, may Israel now say." The wonderful history of his people behind him, so to speak, and the reconquest of their land before him, must have called up the glorious achievements of their fathers, provoking the generous emulation of their sons. The worship was closed by those 700 warriors chanting in magnificent chorus the psalm from which their leader had preached.

To many it seemed significant that here the returned exiles should spend their first Sunday, and resume their sanctuary services. They remembered how this same village of Prali had been the scene of a horrible outrage at the time of their exodus. The Pastor of Prali, M. Leidet, a singularly pious man, had been discovered by the soldiers as he was praying under a rock, and being dragged forth, he was first tortured and mutilated, and then hanged; his last words being, "Lord Jesus, receive my spirit." It was surely appropriate, after the silence of three years and a half, during which the rage of the persecutor had forbidden the preaching of the glorious Gospel, that its re-opening should take place in the pulpit of the martyr Leidet.

CHAPTER 17
Final Re-Establishment in the Valleys

The Vaudois had entered the land, but they had not yet got possession of it. They were a mere handful; they would have to face the large and well-appointed army of Piedmont, aided by the French. But their great leader to his courage added faith. The "cloud" which had guided them over the great mountains, with their snows and abysses, would cover their camp, and lead them forth to battle, and bring them in with victory. It was not surely that they might die in the land, that they had been able to make so marvelous a march back to it. Full of these courageous hopes, the "seven hundred" now addressed themselves to their great task.

They began to climb the Col Julien, which separates Prali from the fertile and central valley of the Waldenses, that of Lucerna. As they toiled up and were now near the summit of the pass, the Piedmontese soldiers, who had been stationed there, shouted out, "Come on, ye Barbets; we guard the pass, and there are 3,000 of us!" They did come on. To force the entrenchments and put to flight the garrison was the work of a moment. In the evacuated camp the Vaudois found a store of ammunition and provisions, which to them was a most seasonable booty. Descending rapidly the slopes and precipices of the great mountain, they surprised and took the town of Bobbio, which nestles at its foot. Driving out the Popish inhabitants to whom it had been made over, they took possession of their ancient dwellings, and paused a little while to rest after the march and conflict of the previous days. Here their second Sunday was passed, and public worship again celebrated, the congregation chanting their psalm to the clash of arms. On the day following, repairing to the "Rock of Sibaud," where their fathers had pledged their faith to God and to one another, they renewed on the same sacred spot their ancient oath, swearing with uplifted hands to abide steadfastly in the profession of the Gospel, to stand by one another, and never to lay down their arms till they had re-established themselves and their brethren in those Valleys which they believed had as really been given to them by the God of heaven as Palestine had been to the Jews.

Their next march was to Villaro, which is situated half-way between Bobbio at the head and La Torre at the entrance of the valley. This town they stormed and took, driving away the new inhabitants. But here their career of conquest was suddenly checked. The next day, a strong reinforcement of regular troops coming up, the Vaudois were under the necessity of abandoning Villaro, and falling back on Bobbio [Monastier, p. 356]. The patriot army now became parted into two bands, and for many weeks had to wage a sort of guerilla war on the mountains. France on the one side, and Piedmont on the other, poured in soldiers, in the hope of exterminating this handful of warriors. The privations and hardships which they endured were as great as the victories which they won in their daily skirmishes were marvelous. But though always conquering, their ranks were rapidly thinning. What though a hundred of the enemy were slain for one Waldensian who fell? The Piedmontese could recruit their numbers, the Vaudois could not add to theirs. They had now neither ammunition nor provisions, save what they took from their enemies; and, to add to their perplexities, winter was near, which would bury their mountains beneath its snows, and leave them without food or shelter. A council of war was held, and it was ultimately resolved to repair to the Valley of Martino, and entrench themselves on La Balsiglia.

This brings us to the last heroic stand of the returned exiles. But first let us sketch the natural strength and grandeur of the spot on which that stand was made. The Balsiglia is situated at the western extremity of San Martino, which in point of grandeur yields to few things in the Waldensian Alps. It is some five miles long by about two in width, having as its floor the richest meadow-land; and for walls, mountains superbly hung with terraces, overflowing with flower and fruitage, and protected above with splintered cliffs and dark peaks. It is closed at the western extremity by the naked face of a perpendicular mountain, down which the Germagnasca is seen to dash in a flood of silver. The meadows and woods that clothe the bosom of the valley are seamed by a broad line of white, formed by the torrent, the bed of which is strewn with so many rocks that it resembles a continuous river of foam.

Than the clothing of the mountains that form the bounding walls of this valley nothing could be finer. On the right, as one advances upwards, rises a succession of terraced vineyards, finely diversified with cornfields and knolls of rock, which are crowned with cottages or hamlets, looking out from amid their rich embowerings of chestnut and apple-tree. Above this fruit-bearing zone are the grassy uplands, the resort of herdsmen, which in their turn give place to the rocky ridges that, in wavy and serrated lines, run off to the higher summits, which recede into the clouds.

On the left the mountain-wall is more steep, but equally rich in its clothing. Swathing its foot is a carpeting of delicious sward. Trees, vast of girth, part, with their over-arching branches, the bright sunlight. Higher up are fields of maize and forests of chestnut; and higher still is seen the rock-loving birch, with its silvery stem and graceful tresses. Along the splintered rocks above runs a bristling line of firs, forming mighty chevaux-de-frise.

Towards the head of the valley, near the vast perpendicular cliff already mentioned, which shuts it in on the west, is seen a glorious assemblage of mountains. One mighty cone uplifts itself above and behind another, till the last and highest buries its top in the rolling masses of cloud, which are seen usually hanging like a canopy above this part of the valley. These noble aiguilles, four in number, rise feathery with firs, and remind one of the fretted pinnacles of some colossal cathedral. This is La Balsiglia. It was on the terraces of this mountain that Henri Arnaud, with his patriot-warriors, pitched his camp, amid the dark tempests of winter, and the yet darker tempests of a furious and armed bigotry. The Balsiglia shoots its gigantic pyramids heavenward, as if proudly conscious of having once been the resting-place of the Vaudois ark. It is no castle of man's erecting; it had for its builder the Almighty Architect himself.

It only remains, in order to complete this picture of a spot so famous in the wars of conscience and liberty, to say that behind the Balsiglia on the west rises the lofty Col du Pis. It is rarely that this mountain permits to the spectator a view of his full stature, for his dark sides run up and bury themselves in the clouds. Face to face with the Col du Pis, stands on the other side of the valley the yet loftier Mont Guinevere, with, most commonly, a veil of cloud around him, as if he too were unwilling to permit to the eye of visitor a sight of his stately proportions. Thus do these two Alps, like twin giants, guard this famous valley.

It was on the lower terrace of this pyramidal mountain, the Balsiglia, that Henri Arnaud--his army now, alas! reduced to 400--sat down. Viewed from the level of the valley, the peak seems to terminate in a point, but on ascending, the top expands into a level grassy plateau. Steep and smooth as escarped fortress, it is unscalable on every side save that on which a stream rushes past from the mountains. The skill of Arnaud enabled him to add to the natural strength of the Vaudois position the defenses of art. They enclosed themselves within earthen walls and ditches; they erected covered ways; they dug out some four-score cellars in the rock, to hold provisions, and they built huts as temporary barracks. Three springs that gushed out of the rock supplied them with water. They constructed similar entrenchments on each of the three peaks that rose above them, so that if the first were taken they could ascend to the second, and so on to the fourth. On the loftiest summit of the Balsiglia, which commanded the entire valley, they placed a sentinel, to watch the movements of the enemy.

Only three days elapsed till four battalions of the French army arrived, and enclosed the Balsiglia on every side. On the 29th of October, an assault was made on the Vaudois position, which was repulsed with great slaughter of the enemy, and the loss of not one man to the defenders. The snows of early winter had begun to fall, and the French general thought it best to postpone the task of capturing the Balsiglia till spring. Destoying all the corn which the Vaudois had collected and stored in the villages, he began his retreat from San Martino, and, taking laconic farewell of the Waldenses, he bade them have patience till Easter, when he would again pay them a visit [Monastier, pp. 304-5].

All through the winter of 1689-90, the Vaudois remained in their mountain fortress, resting after the marches, battles, and sieges of the previous months, and preparing for the promised return of the French. Where Henri Arnaud had pitched his camp, there had he also raised his altar, and if from that mountain-top was pealed forth the shout of battle, from it ascended also, morning and night, the prayer and the psalm. Besides daily devotions, Henri Arnaud preached two sermons weekly, one on Sunday and another on Thursday. At stated times he administered the Lord's Supper. Nor was the commissariat overlooked. Foraging parties brought in wine, chestnuts, apples, and other fruits, which the autumn, now far advanced, had fully ripened. A strong detachment made an incursion into the French valleys of Pragelas and Queyras, and returned with salt, butter, some hundred head of sheep, and a few oxen. The enemy, before departing, had destroyed their stock of grain, and as the fields were long since reaped, they despaired of being able to repair their loss. And yet bread to last them all the winter through had been provided, in a way so marvelous as to convince them that He who feeds the fowls of the air was caring for them. Ample magazines of grain lay all around their encampment, although unknown as yet to them. The snow that year began to fall earlier than usual, and it covered up the ripened corn, which the Popish inhabitants had not time to cut when the approach of the Vaudois compelled them to flee. From this unexpected store-house the garrison drew as they had need. Little did the Popish peasantry, when they sowed the seed in spring, dream that Vaudois hands would reap the harvest.

Corn had been provided for them, and, to Vaudois eyes, provided almost as miraculously as was the manna for the Israelites, but where were they to find the means of grinding it into meal? At almost the foot of the Balsiglia, on the stream of the Germagnasea, is a little mill. The owner, M. Tron-Poulat, three years before, when going forth into exile with his brethren, threw the mill-stone into the river; "for," said he, "it may yet be needed." It was needed now, and search being made for it, it was discovered, drawn out of the stream, and the mill set a-working. There was another and more distant mill at the entrance of the valley, to which the garrison had recourse when the immediate precincts of the Balsiglia were occupied by the enemy and the nearer mill was not available. Both mills exist to this day; their roofs of brown slate may be seen by the visitor, peering up through the luxuriant foliage of the valley, the wheel motionless, it may be, and the torrent which turned it shooting idly past in a volley of spray.

With the return of spring, the army of France and Piedmont reappeared. The Balsiglia was now completely invested, the combined force amounting to 22,000 in all--10,000 French and 12,000 Piedmontese. The troops were commanded by the celebrated De Catinat, lieutenant-general of the armies of France. The "four hundred" Waldenses looked down from their "camp of rock" on the valley beneath them, and saw it glittering with steel by day and shining with camp-fires by night. Catinat never doubted that a single day's fighting would enable him to capture the place; and that the victory, which he looked upon as already won, might be duly celebrated, he ordered four hundred ropes to be sent along with the army, in order to hang at once the four hundred Waldenses; and he had commanded the inhabitants of Pinerolo to prepare feux-de-joie to grace his return from the campaign. The head-quarters of the French were at Great Passet-so called in contradistinction to Little Passet, situated a mile lower in the valley. Great Passet counts some thirty roofs, and is placed on an immense ledge of rock that juts out from the foot of Mont Guinevere, some 800 feet above the stream, and right opposite the Balsiglia. On the flanks of this rocky ledge are still to be seen the ruts worn by the cannon and baggage-wagons of the French army. There can be no doubt that these marks are the memorials of the siege, for no other wheeled vehicles were ever seen in these mountains.*

Having reconnoitered, Catinat ordered the assault (1st May, 1690). Only on that side of Balsiglia where a stream trickles down from the mountains, and which offers a gradual slope, instead of a wall of rock as everywhere else, could the attack be made with any chance of success. But this point Henri Arnaud had taken care to fortify with strong palisades. Five hundred picked men, supported by seven thousand musketeers, advanced to storm the fortress [Monastier, pp. 369,370]. They rushed forward with ardor; they threw themselves upon the palisades; but they found it impossible to tear them down, formed as they were of great trunks,

---

* The Author was conducted over the ground, and had all the memorials of the siege pointed out to him by two most trustworthy and intelligent guides-M. Turin, then Pastor of Macel, whose ancestors had figured in the "Glorious Return;" and the late M. Tron, Syndic of the Commune. The ancestors of M. Tron had returned with Henri Arnaud, and recovered their lands in the Valley of San Martino, and here had the family of M. Tron lived ever since, and the precise spots where the more memorable events of the war had taken place had been handed down from father to son.

fastened by mighty boulders. Massed behind the defense were the Vaudois, the younger men loading the muskets, and the veterans taking steady aim, while the besiegers were falling in dozens at every volley. The assailants beginning to waver, the Waldensians made a fierce sally, sword in hand, and cut in pieces those whom the musket had spared. Of the five hundred picked soldiers only some score lived to rejoin the main body, which had been spectators from the valley of their total rout. Incredible as it may appear, we are nevertheless assured of it as a fact, that not a Vaudois was killed or wounded: not a bullet had touched one of them. The fireworks which Catinat had been so provident as to bid the men of Pinerolo get ready to celebrate his victory were not needed that night.

Despairing of reducing the fortress by other means, the French now brought up cannon, and it was not till the 14th of May that all was ready, and that the last and grand assault was made. Across the ravine in which the conflict we have just described took place, an immense knoll juts out, at an equal level with the lower entrenchments of the Waldenses. To this rock the cannons were hoisted up to play upon the fortress. [Cannon-balls are occasionally picked up in the neighborhood of the Balsiglia. In 1857 the Author was shown one in the Presbytere of Pomaretto, which had been dug up a little before.] Never before had the sound of artillery shaken the rocks of San Martino. It was the morning of Whit-Sunday, and the Waldenses were preparing to celebrate the Lord's Supper, when the first boom from the enemy's battery broke upon their ear [Monastier, p. 371]. All day the cannonading continued, and its dreadful noises, re-echoed from rock to rock, and rolled upwards to the summits of the Col du Pis and the Mont Guinevere, were still further heightened by the thousands of musketeers who were stationed all around the Balsiglia. When night closed in the ramparts of the Waldenses were in ruins, and it was seen that it would not be possible longer to maintain the defense. What was to be done? The cannonading had ceased for the moment, but assuredly the dawn would see the attack renewed.

Never before had destruction appeared to impend so inevitably over the Vaudois. To remain where they were was certain death, yet whither could they flee? Behind them rose the unscalable precipices of the Col du Pis, and beneath them lay the valley swarming with foes. If they should wait till the morning broke it would be impossible to pass the enemy without being seen; and even now, although it was night, the numerous camp-fires that blazed beneath them made it almost as bright as day. But the hour of their extremity was the time of God's opportunity. Often before it had been seen to be so, but perhaps never so strikingly as now. While they looked this way and that way, but could discover no escape from the net that enclosed them, the mist began to gather on the summits of the mountains around them. They knew the old mantle that was wont to be cast around their fathers in the hour of peril. It crept lower and yet lower on the great mountains. Now it touched the supreme peak of the Balsiglia.

Will it mock their hopes? Will it only touch, but not cover, their mountain camp? Again it is in motion; downward roll its white fleecy billows, and now it hangs in sheltering folds around the war-battered fortress and its handful of heroic defenders. They dared not as yet attempt escape, for still the watch-fires burned brightly in the valley. But it was only for a few minutes longer. The mist kept its downward course, and now all was dark. A Tartarean gloom filled the gorge of San Martino.

At this moment, as the garrison stood mute, pondering whereunto these things would grow, Captain Poulat, a native of these parts, broke silence. He bade them be of good courage, for he knew the paths, and would conduct them past the French and Piedmontese lines, by a track known only to himself. Crawling on their hands and knees, and passing close to the French sentinels, yet hidden from them by the mist, they descended frightful precipices, and made their escape. "He who has not seen such paths," says Arnaud in his Rentree Glorieuse, "cannot conceive the danger of them, and will be inclined to consider my account of the march a mere fiction. But it is strictly true; and I must add, the place is so frightful that even some of the Vaudois themselves were terror-struck when they saw by day-light the nature of the spot they had passed in the dark." When the day broke, every eye in the plain below was turned to the Balsiglia. That day the four hundred ropes which Catinat had brought with him were to be put in requisition, and the feux-de-joie so long prepared were to be lighted at Pinerolo. What was their amazement to find the Balsiglia abandoned! The Vaudois had escaped and were gone, and might be seen upon the distant mountains, climbing the snows far out of reach of their would-be captors. Well might they sing-

> "Our soul is escaped as a bird out of the snare of the fowlers.
> The snare is broken, and we are escaped."

There followed several days, during which they wandered from hill to hill, or lay hid in woods, suffering great privations, and encountering numerous perils. At last they succeeded in reaching the Pra del Tor. To their amazement and joy, on arriving at this celebrated and hallowed spot, they found deputies from their prince, the Duke of Savoy, waiting them with an overture of peace. The Vaudois were as men that dreamed. An overture of peace! How was this? A coalition, including Germany, Great Britain, Holland, and Spain, had been formed to check the ambition of France, and three days had been given to Victor Amadeus to say to which side he would join himself-the Leaguers or Louis XIV. He resolved to break with Louis and take part with the coalition. In this case, to whom could he so well commit the keys of the Alps as to his trusty Vaudois? Hence the overture that met them in the Pra del Tor. Ever ready to rally round the throne of their prince the moment the hand of persecution was withdrawn, the Vaudois closed with the peace offered them. Their towns and lands were restored; their churches were reopened for Protestant worship; their brethren still in prison at Turin were liberated, and the colonists of their countrymen in Germany had passports to return to their homes; and thus, after a dreary interval of three and a half years, the Valleys were again peopled with their ancient race, and resounded with their ancient songs. So closed that famous period of their history, which, in respect of the wonders, we might say the miracles, that attended it, we can compare only to the march of the chosen people through the wilderness to the Land of Promise.

CHAPTER 18
Condition of the Waldenses From 1690

With this second planting of the Vaudois in their Valleys, the period of their great persecutions may be said to have come to an end. Their security was not complete, nor their measure of liberty entire. They were still subject to petty oppressions; enemies were never wanting to whisper things to their prejudice; little parties of Jesuits would from time to time appear in their Valleys, the forerunners, as they commonly found them, of some new and hostile edict; they lived in continual apprehension of having the few privileges which had been conceded to them swept away; and on one occasion they were actually threatened with a second expatriation. They knew, moreover, that Rome, the real author of all their calamities and woes, still meditated their extermination, and that she had entered a formal protest against their rehabilitation, and given the duke distinctly to understand that to be the friend of the Vaudois was to be the enemy of the Pope. [Monastier, p. 389. The Pope, Innocent XII., declared (19th August, 1694) the edict of the duke re-establishing the Vaudois null and void, and enjoined his inquisitors to pay no attention to it in their pursuit of the heretics.] Nevertheless their condition was tolerable compared with the frightful tempests which had darkened their sky in previous eras.

The Waldenses had everything to begin anew. Their numbers were thinned; they were bowed down by poverty; but they had vast recuperative power; and their brethren in England and Germany hastened to aid them in reorganizing their Church, and bringing once more into play that whole civil and ecclesiastical economy which the "exile" had so rudely broken in pieces. William III of England incorporated a Vaudois regiment at his own expense, which he placed at the service of the duke, and to this regiment it was mainly owing that the duke was not utterly overwhelmed in his wars with his former ally, Louis XIV. At one point of the campaign, when hard pressed, Victor Amadeus had to sue for the protection of the Vaudois, on almost the very spot where the deputies of Gianavello had sued to him for peace, but had sued in vain.

In 1692 there were twelve churches in the Valleys; but the people were unable to maintain a pastor to each. They were ground down by military imposts. Moreover, a peremptory demand was made upon them for payment of the arrears of taxes which had accrued in respect of their lands during the three years they had been absent, and when to them there was neither seed-time nor harvest. Anything more extortionate could not be imagined. In their extremity, Mary of England, the consort of William III., granted them a "Royal Subsidy," to provide pastors and schoolmasters, and this grant was increased with the increased number of parishes, till it reached the annual sum of 550 pounds. A collection which was made in Great Britain at a subsequent period (1770) permitted an augmentation of the salaries of the pastors. This latter fund bore the name of the "National Subsidy," to distinguish it from the former, the "Royal Subsidy." The States-General of Holland followed in the wake of the English sovereign, and made collections for salaries to schoolmasters, gratuities to superannuated pastors, and for the founding of a Latin school. Nor must we omit to state that the Protestant cantons of Switzerland appropriated bursaries to students from the Valleys at their academies–one at Basle, five at Lausanne, and two at Geneva [Muston, pp. 220-1. Monastier, pp. 388-9].

The policy of the Court of Turin towards the Waldenses changed with the shiftings in the great current of European politics. At one unfavorable moment, when the influence of the Vatican was in the ascendant, Henri Arnaud, who had so gloriously led back the Israel of the Alps, to their ancient inheritance, was banished from the Valleys, along with others, his companions in patriotism and virtue, as now in exile. England, through William, sought to draw the hero to her own shore, but Arnaud retired to Schoenberg, where he spent his last years in the humble and affectionate discharge of the duties of a pastor among his expatriated countrymen, whose steps he guided to the heavenly abodes, as he had done those of their brethren to their earthly land. He died in 1721, at the age of four-score years.

The century passed without any very noticeable event. The spiritual condition of the Vaudois languished. The year 1789 brought with it astounding changes. The French Revolution rung out the knell of the old times, and introduced, amidst those earthquake-shocks that convulsed nations, and laid thrones and altars prostate, a new political age. The Vaudois once again passed under the dominion of France. There followed an enlargement of their civil rights, and an amelioration of their social condition; but, unhappily, with the friendship of France came the poison of its literature, and Voltairianism threatened to inflict more deadly injury on the Church of the Alps than all the persecutions of the previous centuries. At the Restoration the Waldenses were given back to their former sovereign, and with their return to the House of Savoy they returned to their ancient restrictions, though the hand of bloody persecution could no more be stretched out.

The time was now drawing near when this venerable people was to obtain a final emancipation. That great deliverance rose on them, as day rises on the earth, by slow stages. The visit paid them by the apostolic Felix Neff, in 1808, was the first dawning of their new day. With him a breath from heaven, it was felt, had passed over the dry bones. The next stage in their resurrection was the visit of Dr. William Stephen Gilly, in 1828. He cherished, he tells us, the conviction that "this is the spot from which it is likely that the great Sower will again cast his seed, when it shall please him to permit the pure Church of Christ to resume her seat in those Italian States from which Pontifical intrigues have dislodged her" [Waldensian Researches, by William Stephen Gilly, M.A., Prebendary of Durham; p. 158; Lond., 1831]. The result of Dr. Gilly's visit was the erection of a college at La Torre, for the instruction of youth and the training of ministers, and an hospital for the sick; besides awakening great interest on their behalf in England. [So deep was the previous ignorance respecting this people, that Sharon Turner, speaking of the Waldenses in his History of England, placed them on the shores of Lake Leman, confounding the Valleys of the Vaudois with the Canton de Vaud.]

After Dr. Gilly there stood up another to befriend the Waldenses, and prepare them for their coming day of deliverance. The career of General Beckwith is invested with a romance not unlike that which belongs to the life of Ignatius Loyola.

Beckwith was a young soldier, and as brave, and chivalrous, and ambitious of glory as Loyola. He had passed unhurt through battle and siege. He fought at Waterloo till the enemy was in full retreat, and the sun was going down. But a flying soldier discharged his musket at a venture, and the leg of the young officer was hopelessly shattered by the bullet. Beckwith, like Loyola, passed months upon a bed of pain, during which he drew forth from his portmanteau his neglected Bible, and began to read and study it. He had lain down, like Loyola, a knight of the sword, and like him he rose up a knight of the Cross, but in a truer sense.

One day in 1827 he paid a visit to Apsley House, and while he waited for the duke, he took up a volume which was lying on the table. It was Dr. Gilly's narrative of his visit to the Waldenses. Beckwith felt himself drawn irresistibly to a people with whose wonderful history this book made him acquainted for the first time. From that hour his life was consecrated to them. He lived among them as a father-as a king. He devoted his fortune to them. He built schools, and churches, and parsonages. He provided improved school-books, and suggested better modes of teaching. He strove above all things to quicken their spiritual life. He taught them how to respond to the exigencies of modern times. He specially inculcated upon them that the field was wider than their Valleys; and that they would one day be called to arise and to walk through Italy, in the length of it and in the breadth of it. He was their advocate at the court of Turin; and when he had obtained for them the possession of a burying-ground outside their Valleys, he exclaimed, "Now they have got infeftment of Piedmont, as the patriarchs did of Canaan, and soon all the land will be theirs." [The Author may be permitted to bear his personal testimony to the labors of General Beckwith for the Waldenses, and through them for the evangelization of Italy. On occasion of his first visit to the Valleys in 1851, he passed a week mostly in the society of the general, and had details from his own lips of the methods he was pursuing for the elevation of the Church of the Vaudois. All through the Valleys he was revered as a father. His common appellation among them was "The Benefactor of the Vaudois."]

But despite the efforts of Gilly and Beckwith, and the growing spirit of toleration, the Waldenses continued to groan under a load of political and social disabilities. They were still a proscribed race.

The once goodly limits of their Valleys had, in later times, been greatly contracted, and like the iron cell in the story, their territory was almost yearly tightening its circle round them. They could not own, or even farm, a foot-breadth of land, or practice any industry, beyond their own boundary. They could not bury their dead save in the Valleys; and when it chanced that any of their people died at Turin or elsewhere, their corpses had to be carried all the way to their own graveyards. They were not permitted to erect a tombstone above their dead, or even to enclose their burial-grounds with a wall. They were shut out from all the learned and liberal professions-they could not be bankers, physicians, or lawyers. No avocation was left them but that of tending their herds and pruning their vines. When any of them emigrated to Turin, or other Piedmontese town, they were not permitted to be anything but domestic servants. There was no printing-press in their Valleys-they were forbidden to have one; and the few books they possessed, mostly Bibles, catechisms, and hymn-books, were printed abroad, chiefly in Great Britain; and when they arrived at La Torre, the Moderator had to sign before the Reviser-in-Chief an engagement that not one of these books should be sold, or even lent, to a Roman Catholic [General Beckwith: his Life and Labors, &c. By J.P. Meille, Pastor of the Waldensian Church at Turin. P. 26. Lond., 1873].

They were forbidden to evangelize or make converts. But though fettered on the one side they were not equally protected on the other, for the priests had full liberty to enter their Valleys, and proselytize; and if a boy of twelve or a girl of ten professed willingness to enter the Roman Church, they were to be taken from their parents, that they might with the more freedom carry out their intention. They could not marry save among their own people. They could not erect a sanctuary save on the soil of their own territory. They could take no degree at any of the colleges of Piedmont. In short, the duties, rights, and privileges that constitute life they were denied. They were reduced as nearly as was practicable to simple existence, with this one great exception-which was granted them not as a right, but as a favor-namely, the liberty of Protestant worship within their territorial limits.

The Revolution of 1848, with trumpet-peal, sounded the overthrow of all these restrictions. They fell in one day. The final end of Providence in preserving that people during long centuries of fearful persecutions now began to be seen. The

Waldensian Church became the door by which freedom of conscience entered Italy. When the hour came for framing a new constitution for Piedmont, it was found desirable to give standing-room in that constitution to the Waldenses, and this necessitated the introduction into the edict of the great principle of freedom of worship as a right. The Waldenses had contended for that principle for ages-they had maintained and vindicated it by their sufferings and martyrdoms; and therefore they were necessitated to demand, and the Piedmontese Government to grant, this great principle. It was the only one of the many new constitutions framed for Italy at that same time in which freedom of conscience was enacted. Now would it have found a place in the Piedmontese constitution, but for the circumstance that here were the Waldenses, and that their great distinctive principle demanded legal recognition, otherwise they would remain outside the constitution. The Vaudois alone had fought the battle, but all their countrymen shared with them the fruits of the great victory. When the news of the Statuto of Carlo Alberto reached La Torre there were greetings on the streets, psalms in the churches, and blazing bonfires at night on the crest of the snowy Alps.

At the door of her Valleys, with lamp in hand, its oil unspent and its light unextinguished, is seen, at the era of 1848, the Church of the Alps, prepared to obey the summons of her heavenly King, who has passed by in earthquake and whirlwind, casting down the thrones that of old oppressed her, and opening the doors of her ancient prison. She is now to go forth and be "The Light of all Italy" ["Totius Italiae lumen"], as Dr. Gilly, thirty years before, had foretold she would at no distant day become. Happily not all Italy as yet, but only Piedmont, was opened to her. She addressed herself with zeal to the work of erecting churches and forming congregations in Turin and other towns of Piedmont. Long a stranger to evangelistic work, the Vaudois Church had time and opportunity thus given her to acquire the mental courage and practical habits needed in the novel circumstances in which she was now placed. She prepared evangelists, collected funds, organized colleges and congregations, and in various other ways perfected her machinery in anticipation of the wider field that Providence was about to open to her.

It is now the year 1859, and the drama which had stood still since 1849 begins once more to advance. In that year France declared war against the Austrian occupation of the Italian peninsula. The tempest of battle passes from the banks of the Po to those of the Adige, along the plain of Lombardy, rapid, terrible, and decisive as the thunder-cloud of the Alps, and the Tedeschi retreat before the victorious arms of the French. The blood of the three great battles of the campaign was scarcely dry before Austrian Lombardy, Modena, Parma, Tuscany, and part of the Pontifical States had annexed themselves to Piedmont, and their inhabitants had become fellow-citizens of the Waldenses. With scarcely a pause there followed the brilliant campaign of Garibaldi in Sicily and Naples, and these rich and ample territories were also added to the now magnificent kingdom of Victor Emmanuel. The whole of Italy, from the Alps to Etna, the "States of the Church" excepted, now became the field of the Waldensian Church. Nor was this field the end of the drama. Another ten years pass away: France again sends forth her armies to battle, believing that she can command victory as aforetime. The result of the brief but terrible campaign of 1870, in which the French Empire disappeared and the German uprose, was the opening of the gates of Rome. And let us mark-for in the little incident we hear the voice of ten centuries-in the first rank of the soldiers whose cannon had burst upon the old gates, there enters a Vaudois colporteur with a bundle of Bibles. The Waldenses now kindle their lamp at Rome, and the purpose of the ages stands revealed!

Epilogue

The faith of the Waldensians has persevered into this post-modern age, though in forms somewhat different from the past. In the twentieth century, the Waldensian Evangelical Church developed and spread through Italy, gaining converts by building schools in poor areas. The Waldensians also worked to save Jews during Nazi Germany's World War II occupation of northern Italy, hiding many of them in the same mountain valley where their own Waldensian ancestors found refuge.

Waldensians also made homes in the western hemisphere. During American colonial times many Waldensians found freedom in North America's Atlantic shores. Waldensians established early settlements in New Jersey and Delaware. By the late 1800s many Waldensians arrived in the United States with other Italian immigrants. They founded communities in New York City, Chicago, Monett, Galveston and Rochester. In 1893, Waldensians migrated from the Cottian Alps region of Northern Italy to North Carolina and founded the most notable Waldensian settlement in North America: Valdese, North Carolina. The city is home to the Waldensian Presbyterian Church, who operate the Waldensian Heritage Museum.   Waldensians also settled in South America, where today as many as 40 congregations and 15,000 members of the Waldensian Evangelical Church make their homes in Uruguay and Argentina.

Today, the Waldensian Church is included in the Alliance of Reformed Churches of the Presbyterian Order. The Waldensian Church of the twenty-first century considers itself to be a Christian Protestant church of the Reformed tradition, a system and approach to the Christian life that emphasizes the sovereignty of God over all things. The organization is governed by an annual synod, and the affairs of the individual congregations are administered by a board of leaders from the local congregation (consistory) under the presidency of the pastor.

Other Protestant sects attribute their origins to the faithfulness of the Waldensians, including Anabaptists, Baptists and Seventh-day Adventists. Ellen G. White, a founding member of the Seventh-day Adventist movement, taught that the Waldenses were preservers of biblical truth during the great apostasy of the Roman Catholic Church, with many observing the seventh-day Sabbath as a sign of their loyalty to the Creator and Savior, and opposition to the Roman church's self-appointed day of worship, Sunday.

Editor

QUICK ORDER FORM

Order additional copies for your friends and family.

Internet Orders: http://www.MustardSeedImprints.com
E-mail Orders: orders@MustardSeedImprints.com
Postal Orders: Mustard Seed Imprints, PO Box 1211, Clackamas, OR 97015

Name: _____

Mailing Address: _____

City: _____

State: _____ **ZIP:** _____

Telephone: _____ **Email:** _____

Quantity	Title	Cost	Total Quantity x Cost
	PAULA THE WALDENSIAN	$14.95	
	LET IT SHINE: THE HISTORY OF THE WALDENSES	$14.95	
	U.S. Media Mail Shipping *	$3.50	
	Total Enclosed		

*Please contact us by e-mail or purchase on our website for international or express shipping.

Free Bible Lessons at
Bibleinfo.com

QUICK ORDER FORM

Order additional copies for your friends and family.

Internet Orders: http://www.MustardSeedImprints.com
E-mail Orders: orders@MustardSeedImprints.com
Postal Orders: Mustard Seed Imprints, PO Box 1211, Clackamas, OR 97015

Name: _____

Mailing Address: _____

City: _____

State: _____ **ZIP:** _____

Telephone: _____ **Email:** _____

Quantity	Title	Cost	Total Quantity x Cost
	PAULA THE WALDENSIAN	$11.95	
	LET IT SHINE: THE HISTORY OF THE WALDENSES	$11.95	
	U.S. Media Mail Shipping *	$3.50	
		Total Enclosed	

*Please contact us by e-mail or purchase on our website for international or express shipping.

Free Bible Lessons at
Bibleinfo.com

www.ingramcontent.com/pod-product-compliance
Lightning Source LLC
Chambersburg PA
CBHW020001050426
42450CB00005B/270